Seeking the Savior

SpiritLed Woman Magazine presents selections
from over 20 of today's most popular Christian writers,
plus a 30-Day Prayer and Revival Devotional.

Seeking the Savior

FAMILY CHRISTIAN STORES

www.FamilyChristian.com

Published by Family Christian Stores, 5300 Patterson Avenue SE,
Grand Rapids, Michigan 49530.

ISBN 1593910002

1 2 3 4 5 6 7 8 9 10

Stregthen Your Heart | Renew Your Mind | Restore Your Soul

Dear Valued Guest,

For more than seventy years, Family Christian Stores has had the privilege of impacting lives for Christ as a ministry-minded business. For this reason, we take extra care to offer one of the widest selections of Christian products designed to strengthen the hearts, minds and souls of believers and seekers from all ages and stages of life. This book you now hold in your hand is an extension of our mission. The Hearts, Minds & Souls series is an exclusive collection of books created to engage our guests in transforming and redemptive relationships with our Savior, Jesus Christ.

In addition to this book, the over ten thousand different products available in our stores and through FamilyChristian.com website provide a wealth of additional resources to address every need from a faith-filled, Christ-centered perspective. We have Bibles for everyone from young children just learning to read to seminary students serious about every nuance of Greek and Hebrew. We even have Bible accessories like covers, highlighters, tabs and more. We have books for men and women, singles and married couples, kids, tweens, teens and adults. We have music to minister to the hearts of every rhyme and rhythmical preference. From cards to tees, household items to framed art, pens to games, whatever your need, we promise you'll find something to enrich and enhance your lifestyle at Family Christian Stores.

We're also sensitive to your desire to be a good steward of the resources God has given you. That's why we offer a price matching promise, exclusive Perks program and great monthly deals on the latest most popular books and music.

Thank you for shopping Family Christian Stores and FamilyChristian.com. We appreciate your partnership in reaching families and communities with the gospel and grace of Jesus Christ. We ask that you pray for us as we seek to operate our company in a way that best fulfills the mission God has given us.

Answering the call to help strengthen
the hearts, minds & souls of our guests,

Dave Browne
President/CEO
Family Christian Stores

Strengthen Your Heart

May he strengthen your hearts so that you
will be blameless and holy in the presence
of our God and Father when our Lord
Jesus comes with all his holy ones.

1 Thessalonians 3:13

WHO IS THIS JESUS?
by Larry Tomczak

Knowing the facts about Christ is not the same as loving Him intimately.

During the 19th century, liberal theologians began a search to rediscover the historical Jesus. They were intent on determining the true personality of a Jesus who existed 2,000 years earlier. Leading this pursuit was Dr. Albert Schweitzer, the Nobel Peace Prize-winning philosopher, theologian and medical missionary.

The fruit of his work was disclosed in his highly acclaimed book *The Quest of the Historical Jesus*, which was released in 1906—the same year the Azusa Street Revival lit the world on fire.

After exhaustive research, Schweitzer concluded that Jesus was a mysterious, power-hungry ruler who arrogantly considered Himself the Son of Man. Titles such as Messiah, Son of Man and Son of God, Schweitzer said, were merely "historical parables," and Jesus' claims of divinity were not based on reality. Schweitzer wrote, "We can find no designation that expresses what He is for us."

In Schweitzer's opinion, Jesus had nothing in common with contemporary society, but He could be known through individual experience. For Schweitzer that meant running a hospital in Africa. Although he helped a great deal of people and was truly sincere—Schweitzer was sincerely wrong.

He sought the Jesus of 2,000 years ago rather than the Jesus of today. The tools of his research were human intellect, the scientific method and subjective experience rather than Scripture, prayer and meditation.

☞ You Can Know Jesus Through the Bible

How important is it to rediscover the Jesus of the Bible? I venture to say it means everything. However, revelation—which doesn't come from human intellect or scientific method—is at the core of who Jesus is. Revelation is the process God uses to show the beauty and power of Jesus in your life through the Word of God.

When you know the Jesus of the Bible, you daily fall more and more in love with Him. Jesus doesn't want you following Him out of cold, rigid, legalistic obedience as if He were an impersonal taskmaster or an exacting judge. He wants you to obey Him because you love Him and delight in pleasing Him!

Yes, He is a monarch and righteous ruler, but He is foremost a loving Lord who laid down His life for you and continues to pray for you every day before the Father (SEE HEB. 7:25). In fact, He desires to relate to you as a Bridegroom with His bride. Jesus wants you captivated, fascinated and exhilarated by a true revelation of Him, by truly "knowing" Him.

To know Jesus, you must begin with the Bible. The Bible was written to introduce you to a Person—Jesus. By wholeheartedly believing in Him, you can share eternity with Him. In the closing words of his Gospel, John wrote, "But these are written that you may believe that Jesus is the Christ, the Son of God, and that by believing you may have life in His name" (JOHN 20:31, NIV).

For many Christians, believing in Jesus the Son of God is much easier than believing in Jesus the Son of Man—a real, live person. Without forfeiting any of His divinity, Jesus came to Earth and clothed Himself with human skin.

But after His resurrection, Jesus didn't stop being a man. Jesus did not temporarily become a man (the incarnation) for a season and then return to heaven, dissolve His humanity and "go back to being only God." The eternal, uncreated, omnipotent, omniscient, omnipresent second Person of the Trinity became a man and will remain a man forever!

Relating to a personal God who is a literal Person is so much easier than relating to some "beatific vision" or "ethereal presence." Unfortunately, a great deal of religious training not only distorts the personality of Jesus but also ignores His humanity in attempting to emphasize His divinity. We need both! By building a friendship with the man Christ Jesus, you build a relationship with Jesus, the Son of God.

ℬ *An Interesting Romance*

During the 1870s two unbelievers sat on a railroad train discussing the life of Christ. Both were skeptical attorneys: one a writer, the other a famous agnostic. "I think an interesting romance could be written about Him," the writer commented. His friend replied, "And you are just the man to write it. Tear down the prevailing sentiment about His divinity and paint Him as a man."

The writer, former Civil War general Lewis Wallace, accepted his friend's challenge. Yet the challenge didn't come from an unknown agnostic attorney. It came from a noted opponent of Christianity, Robert Ingersoll, whose scurrilous attacks on biblical belief commanded up to $3,500 for one lecture—a hefty sum in those days.

In the process of constructing the history of Christ, Wallace found himself facing the greatest life ever lived on Earth. The more he studied the Bible, the more he was convinced. He fell in love with the compassionate Savior.

His heart was so captivated that one day he felt compelled to cry, "Truly this was the Son of God." He finished the book, and it eventually became the all-time classic *Ben-Hur*.

Meet the Real Jesus! God wants you to know the love of Christ. He wants you to drink deeply of His love and discover the beauty, the reality of His only begotten Son, who is "beautiful beyond description."

The Bible says that God loves you and delights in you so much that in spite of your shortcomings and sins He bursts forth in heartfelt song! If you are a Christian, the wrath of God is no longer upon you. He's not mad at you anymore—He's on your side!

In fact, Scripture says He not only saves you; He also sings over you! "On that day they will say to Jerusalem, 'Do not fear, O Zion; do not let your hands hang limp. The Lord your God is with you, He is mighty to save. He will take great delight in you, He will quiet you with his love, He will rejoice over you with singing'" (ZEPH. 3:16-17).

Believe it or not, God enjoys you. He not only loves you; He likes you too and wants to spend time with you. He wants you to follow Him out of sheer delight, captivated by the compelling personality and character of His one and only Son.

The real Jesus is full of life and joy, and He loves you extravagantly. In the deep recesses of every heart, Jesus whispers, "Come. Stop trying to fill the hole in your heart with things that cannot satisfy. Drink of My love and find true life." A love relationship with Jesus is the foundation of your very life.

Jesus is the Bridegroom who ravishes His bride, the church, with His love. This same Jesus ravishes you with His love. Jesus wants a full-time bride—not some part-time girlfriend!

To see yourself as part of a bridal party is not about gender but position. He longs to be with you as a bridegroom longs to be with His bride! It is this joyful Jesus who, as a bridegroom, beckons you to follow Him as His beloved bride.

Who is this person who calls you to Himself? It's the festive Jesus who enjoys celebrating a wedding feast; the servant Jesus who prepares a seaside breakfast for His men; the masculine Jesus whom brawny fishermen follow unashamedly. It is the pure Jesus whom hypocritical leaders despise and the joyful Jesus whose infectious smile melts the hearts of the multitudes.

ꙮ *The Jesus of My First Love*

The Jesus I am describing is the Jesus who won my heart when I was much younger. After 20 years of emptiness, which included 12 years of religious schooling, I discovered that true Christianity is not based on religious rules. It is based on a living, dynamic relationship with Jesus Christ.

Up to that point in my life I had searched everywhere for peace and purpose. Then someone introduced me to Jesus. Scales lifted from my eyes and I realized that Christianity was not about performance or production—it was about a Person!

I was overwhelmed by the real Jesus of the Bible, and I embraced a relationship with the One who created me and laid down His life for me so that I could experience His abundant life (SEE JOHN 10:10).

Over time, however, I strayed from my love relationship with Jesus. The tendency after experiencing a true revelation of Him is to replace intimacy with ministry, passion for the Lord of the work with production for the work of the Lord. While Jesus was calling me back to emulating Mary, I was stuck mimicking Martha (SEE LUKE 10:38-42).

I needed to discover Jesus again. I needed to leap off the treadmill of performance and pressure, back into the loving arms of the smiling Shepherd I once knew.

In the closing hours of her life, Eileen Wallis (wife of one of England's premier prophets and church leaders, Arthur Wallis) gave me this counsel: "Enjoy Jesus, Larry. Take time to simply enjoy being with Him."

How about you? Are you enjoying your relationship with Jesus Christ, or have you slipped from sheer delight in Him to drudgery, activity and more and more ministry?

If your hunger to spend time communing with Jesus has decreased, if your experiences of God's faithfulness are limited to stories of the past, or if you continually struggle to win victory over battles that stand in your way, you may need to rediscover Jesus.

☞ Rekindling Your First Love

Jesus once spoke to a group of believers who had become settled in their relationship with Him: "'I know your deeds, your hard work and your perseverance. I know that you cannot tolerate wicked men, that you have tested those who claim to be apostles but are not, and have found them false.

'You have persevered and have endured hardships for my name, and have not grown weary. Yet I hold this against you: You have forsaken your first love'" (REV. 2:2-4).

The Christians in Ephesus weren't bad people. They opposed wickedness; they tested all teaching with the truth of God's Word; and they refused to give up under persecution. From outward appearances these people would be considered solid Christians—and they were. Yet, Jesus said, "You have forsaken your first love."

If you can identify with these solid believers, then this Scripture passage gives three simple keys that can help you rekindle your passion for Jesus.

～ Remember. Think back to the former days when you enjoyed the sweetness of Jesus' presence and favor.

～ Repent. In prayer, confess that you have allowed yourself to stray from your first love. Ask for forgiveness, and choose to turn around and return to Jesus.

～ Repeat. Do again those simple things you did to cultivate your relationship with Jesus. Read your Bible and spend consistent quality time with Him in worship, prayer and meditation. Remember He likes you, He longs for you—in spite of your short-comings and sin.

Respond to Jesus. Be motivated not by guilt and pressure but by His deep-seated, passionate devotion to you! "We love [Him] because He first loved us," John says *(1 JOHN 4:19)*. What a joy it is to rediscover Jesus and be rekindled in bridal affection for Him as the "Lover of our soul." ❀

 Larry Tomczak is senior pastor of Christ the King Church of Greater Atlanta and executive director of Christ the King School of Ministry. He has authored six books, including Reckless Abandon, *published by Charisma House, from which this article is adapted.*

FOR FURTHER STUDY ON THIS TOPIC:

RECKLESS ABANDON
BY LARRY TOMCZAK (CHARISMA HOUSE)

THE JESUS I NEVER KNEW
BY PHILIP YANCEY (ZONDERVAN)

NO WONDER THEY CALL HIM THE SAVIOR
BY MAX LUCADO (MULTNOMAH)

CALLED TO BE HIS BRIDE
by Mike Bickle

Our understanding of the kingdom of God takes a dramatic turn when we realize our first calling is to love and enjoy Jesus.

What would God preach to the human race if He knew He had only one more sermon? We can find the answer simply by turning in our Bibles to Matthew 21 and 22. Here the Holy Spirit records Jesus' last public sermon—a message filled with mystery, surprise and profound significance for the church today.

"'The kingdom of heaven,'" Jesus said, "'is like a certain king who arranged a marriage for his son'" (Matt. 22:2, NKJV).

These words exploded from the Lord's heart only days before He went to the cross. Up to that time, He had compared the kingdom of God to many things in His parables and teachings. Now He presented one final paradigm: the kingdom of God as a wedding feast.

Why did He save this theme until last? I believe Jesus was enticing His people with a dynamic new emphasis on divine romance, knowing it would excite the human heart as nothing else would. He wanted to stir up a hot desire in each of us for extravagant "bridegroom love," with Jesus Himself as the Bridegroom, and we, His people, His church, the cherished bride.

The prophet Hosea, in approximately 750 B.C., saw this paradigm coming. Speaking prophetically about how the redeemed would view the Messiah in the generation of the Lord's return, he wrote: "'And it shall be, in that day,' says the Lord, 'that you will call Me "my Husband"'" (Hos. 2:16).

Similarly, the apostle Paul wrote, "Husbands, love your wives, just as Christ also loved the church and gave Himself for her. 'For this reason a man shall leave his father and mother and be joined to his wife, and the two shall become one flesh.' This is a great mystery, but I speak concerning Christ and the church" (Eph. 5:25,31-32).

The Holy Spirit then closed the written Word with this same bridal theme: "And the Spirit and the bride say, 'Come!'" *(Rev. 22:17)*.

☞ *Our Spiritual Identity*

Over the years, other kingdom comparisons have captured the church's attention, revealing a corresponding truth about our spiritual identity: We are the family of God, the army of God, the body of Christ, a royal priesthood. But I believe the bridal paradigm is coming to the forefront at this time in church history because of its unique impact on the human heart. Before the second coming of Christ, the Holy Spirit will emphasize a revelation of the Messiah as our Bridegroom God, and our spiritual identity will be transformed into one of a cherished, lovesick bride.

The emotional implications are vast. Not only will the first commandment—"You shall love the Lord your God with all your heart, with all your soul, and with all your mind" *(Matt. 22:37)*—be restored to its primary role in the church, but many of the ways we operate within our own hearts and with each other will change as we see Jesus as our heavenly Bridegroom.

For one, our efforts to fulfill the Great Commission will be less bruising. The reality is that when we work hard for God without being tenderized by the love of God, we often end up bruised, broken and burned out. We were never meant to function best as workers for God; rather, God designed us in His image to be lovers of God!

When we seek first to be extravagant lovers of Jesus, a dynamic of the Spirit is released in our inner man. We carry its reward in us: a lovesick heart fascinated with the beauty of Christ Jesus. In fact, our primary reward in this life is this ability to feel God's love—to be tenderized by His love for us and then to be exhilarated with love back to Him.

Only as lovesick worshipers are we able to maintain an overflowing heart toward God even in difficult circumstances.

Sacrifices of obedience that were once a burden take on a new sweetness. People may treat us wrongly, and life may get tough.

But if we have a fascinated, lovesick heart, our natural circumstances won't dominate our lives.

Sadly, many of us in the church today seek God for other things: more anointing for ministry, economic prosperity, favor with people. These are certainly blessings from God, but they were always designed to be secondary. When they become primary, our spiritual life is weakened. As the Holy Spirit reveals the bridal paradigm in the last days, I'm convinced the primary reward of the kingdom—the ability to experience God's love and love Him back—will come increasingly to the forefront in the hearts and minds of believers.

☙ An Impartation of Love

Of course, it takes God to love God. But God the Father is pleased to impart His love into the heart of the redeemed. In His final high priestly prayer, Jesus said, in essence, "'Father, put the same love with which You love Me, in them!'" (see John 17:26). I believe the Father must have answered Him: "Son, You can be sure that I will impart to them the same fiery love I have for You. It will be done."

Amazingly, we are the designated beneficiaries of that prayer! God wants to give each of us an impartation of His divine love. He wants to induct us into the "fellowship of the burning heart."

The three Persons of the Trinity have burning hearts of love for One Another. It is almost beyond comprehension that God beckons each of us—along with the redeemed throughout human history—into this fellowship.

The experience of holy affection brings us to the highest, most exhilarating heights known in the created order. Oh, the glory of possessing fiery affections!

The capacity to feel deeply and love passionately is truly one of the great expressions of being created in God's image. Of course, this capacity can be dangerous and destructive if not stewarded properly. But the capacity to burn with deep desire in the heart is what separates us from the rest of creation.

God wants His people, by His grace, to emerge as voluntary lovers of God. The bride of Christ is the crowning glory of His creation—far below the transcendent God in glory, yet exalted beyond the angelic host in intimacy with Jesus. And though our bridal position is the highest in all created order, it is never to be confused with being equal to God. Cult groups blur this vital distinction.

The Father has ordained that His Son have an eternal partner who is equally yoked to Him in love. This is possible only because it is God's own love that is given to us for Jesus.

☙ Lovers, Not Workers

Grasping our identity—that of voluntary lovers who will live forever cherished by Jesus as His bride—will change our whole approach to ministry and service. We will no longer see ourselves merely as God's messengers or as servants fulfilling an important task. Rather, out of a lovesick heart, we will find ourselves empowered by love to do the work of the kingdom.

This will be the characteristic of the martyrs at the end of the age: Lost in love, they won't care what they are called to do; they'll just want to do it with Him! They will want to love and obey Him whether in this age or in the age to come, whether in heaven or on earth. Their hearts will be reaching for that primary reward: to live overflowing in the experience of the love of God— to experience love from Him, to love back and to love others with the overflow.

This is the key to unity in the church, and it will be the key to bringing in the great harvest. Ultimately, the Great Commission will be fulfilled by people lovesick for God and thus overflowing with compassion for other people.

Lovers are always more effective than mere workers. Workers have limits to which they will go for the one they serve; lovers don't. My brother broke his neck at a high school football game 25 years ago. He's been totally paralyzed ever since, and I've been in and out of different institutions with him during the years.

One marvelous thing I've seen, every now and then, is a nurse who falls in love with her patient. At that point, she becomes a lover and not just a worker. She delights to go above and beyond the call of duty.

When workers become lovers, they throw away the obligatory checklist. They no longer need it. Their lovesick hearts provide a higher and more trustworthy rule to live and work by. When that happens between us and our heavenly Bridegroom, there will be no self-congratulation or religious self-determination in our efforts to serve Him—only an overflow of love.

When we extravagantly obey God out of a fascinated, exhilarated heart, we come to the position of the bride in Song of Solomon, who pursues her Bridegroom out of "lovesickness" (SEE SONG 2:5; 5:8). While this love song speaks of the beauty of natural married love, a second and important interpretation reveals the beauty of spiritual love for Jesus. It is a picture of the relationship between Christ and His church. In the last days God is going to cause the church—despite tribulations and persecutions—to possess a glad, exhilarated heart rooted in lovesickness for her Bridegroom, Jesus.

☙ *The Beauty of God*

The beauty of God is the ultimate fascination of the bride. Isaiah 4:2 says, "The Branch of the Lord shall be beautiful and glorious." This speaks of the Holy Spirit's emphasis on the beauty of Jesus at the end of the age.

The human race has a longing for fascination and beauty; we can neither repent of it nor quench it. The secular entertainment industry has exploited this longing, providing us with a fascination that not only breaks us but causes us to be dependent upon it— so that we come back for more of that which destroys.

The truth is that when we're not wholehearted or fascinated, we're vulnerable to temptation. The church in the Western world right now is suffering from chronic boredom and passivity. We're vulnerable to the enticements of entertainment and sin. But the bridal paradigm offers the antidote: All our longings to be fascinated will be satisfied as God reveals Himself as our Bridegroom in the divine romance.

The invitation to be the bride of Christ is a unique privilege for the redeemed that far surpasses the position of the angels. It is not a matter of being male or female. Just as women are "sons of God," so also men are the "bride of Christ."

The bridal position describes a relationship of nearness to the heart of God and insight into the beauty of God that transcends gender. Consider King David, the most lovesick man in the Old Testament.

Struck with the beauty of God, he wrote, "One thing I have desired of the Lord, that will I seek: that I may dwell in the house of the Lord all the days of my life, to behold the beauty of the Lord" (Ps. 27:4). David never lost that sense of fascination and awe with the One he loved—the One who first loved him.

When we begin to see Jesus as our Bridegroom, we will no longer consider ourselves task-doers who sacrifice to obey a distant God; nor will we define ourselves by our struggle and our sin. We'll be lovers of God—even while we're struggling. We will say, "I'm a lover of God! Yes, I acknowledge my weakness, but I'm more than a sinful servant. I'm the bride of Christ."

The fact is, a wedding is set to take place at the end of natural history—the culmination of a divine romance more exciting, more exhilarating, than anything the world has ever imagined. Jesus, our Bridegroom, loves us with a fiery love that will last for all eternity. As the bride of Christ, let us make ourselves ready. ❧

Mike Bickle is the director of the International House of Prayer of Kansas City, Missouri (www.fotb.com), a 24-hour-a-day prayer ministry in the spirit of the Tabernacle of David.

FOR FURTHER STUDY ON THIS TOPIC:

THE GOD CHASERS
BY TOMMY TENNEY (DESTINY IMAGE)

THE SONG OF THE BRIDE
BY JEANNE GUYON (CHRISTIAN BOOKS)

INTIMACY WITH THE BELOVED
BY PAT CHEN (CHARISMA HOUSE)

THE HEART OF A WORSHIPER
by Fuchsia Pickett

In order to experience worship in spirit and truth, we must surrender our hearts completely to the lordship of Christ.

Shortly after I was healed from a life-threatening disease and baptized in the Holy Spirit, I was asked to minister in a Pentecostal church. There I was introduced to a dimension of worship that I had never experienced before.

Sitting on the platform in my studied dignity as a former Methodist professor, observing the worship service that was so different from that to which I was accustomed, I was fascinated by all that was going on around me. Though their worship expression seemed disorderly—almost irreverent—in comparison with Methodist tradition, I could tell these people deeply loved the Lord and were expressing their love to Him.

I looked down from my seat on the platform and saw a pretty red-headed woman standing with her hands raised and her eyes closed worshiping God. She was perhaps 35 years old. Her face glowed as if it reflected a thousand-watt lightbulb. Tears were flowing down her cheeks, and I heard her say, "I love You, Jesus."

As I watched her, it seemed to me that her face got brighter and brighter. I couldn't hear everything she was saying from where I was, and I was curious. So I walked down off the platform and stood in front of her. She ignored me.

I leaned over and said, "You and the Lord are having a good time, aren't you, Honey?" Still she didn't pay attention to me. I was insulted. I thought, Doesn't she know I am the guest evangelist?

I heard her say: "You are the Lily of the Valley. I love You. You are the Bright and Morning Star." I recognized that she was quoting love phrases from the Song of Solomon. She continued, "Thank You for being my husband, my friend." Somewhat awed, I went back to the platform.

But I could not take my eyes off her. I knew she was experiencing the presence of God in a way that I never had. I watched her awhile, then walked back down to stand by her.

She did not know I was there. So I returned to the platform a second time. Still watching her, I thought, Maybe she doesn't hear well.

I walked down a third time and stood behind her so I could speak into her ear. Again I said, "You and the Lord are having a good time together, aren't you?"

What I really wanted to say was: "What is going on? I don't understand what it is you are enjoying." I thought she could explain it to me, but still she did not acknowledge my presence.

This time when I returned to the platform I felt someone punch me. I recognized that it was the Lord trying to get my attention. He spoke to me so sweetly, "Fuchsia, you can have that if you want it." I didn't even know what "that" was, but I assumed He was referring to my fascination with the young worshiper.

I went to my room after the service and got on my knees. I said to the Lord: "All right, what is it? You said I could have the thing that made that girl so 'lost' she didn't know I was there. What is that?"

The Lord answered, "I seek a people who worship Me in spirit and truth."

I asked, "Is that worship? Then what have I been doing all these years?"

"Without this revelation of worship," He replied gently, "you have simply been having religious services."

"How can I have that?" I cried out.

☞ *Revelation of Worship*

Then the Lord asked me three simple questions. First He inquired, "What would you do if you had just heard the gates of heaven click behind your heels, and you knew you were through with the devil forever?"

I responded, "I would shout, 'Glory!'"

He said, "Shout it." And I did.

I told Him that I would cry, "Hallelujah!"

He said, "Do it." And I did.

Then He asked me what I would do if I looked up and saw Jesus for the first time.

I said that I would bow at His feet, kiss His nail-scarred hands and wash His feet with my tears.

He said, "Do it."

I meditated on the efficacious, vicarious, substitutionary and mediatorial work of Calvary, and suddenly I experienced a fresh glimpse of the Lamb of God. I began to bow before the Lamb who was slain, but He asked me to look up into His face. "When you see Me face to face," He asked, "what will you tell Me?"

When I heard those words, it was as if a dam within my soul broke, allowing torrents of praise to flood my lips. I told Him how wonderful He was. I recited the attributes of God I had learned in Bible college. When I finished, He asked me if these were the only adjectives I had for Him.

With a sense of awe I responded simply, "You are wonderful."

A picture came to my mind, and I saw the face of Jesus before me as if it were framed. Then the frame faded. As I looked into His face, I told Him how much I loved Him. I had never done that in my life. I told Him how precious He was to me. I went on and on, trying to express my love for Him with my limited vocabulary.

When I was answering His three questions, it seemed as if just a few moments had passed. But it had actually been an hour and a half since I first knelt there. For the first time in my life I had been in the presence of God in such a way that I had lost all consciousness of time. I had begun to experience true worship—my heart responding to the love of God and expressing adoration and love to Him. All my years of Bible training, study and ministry had not evoked the response of worship from my heart that a few moments of divine revelation in His presence had.

As a sincere Methodist professor and pastor, I had thought I understood what worship of an omnipotent God involved, and I regarded our worship services as important expressions of true reverence for God—the creature worshiping his Creator. Though we did honor God sincerely from our hearts, I now understand that we had defined worship very narrowly according to the tradition of our church fathers.

My renewed study of the Scriptures concerning worship has helped me understand the divine destiny each of us has to become worshippers. Much of what is written in my book *Worship Him* (CREATION HOUSE) is what I have learned as I have allowed my Teacher, the blessed Holy Spirit, to open my spiritual eyes to the purpose of God for our personal fulfillment—to become worshippers of God in spirit and in truth.

When I searched the Scriptures with this purpose in mind, many passages I had read before and thought I understood doctrinally began to live in my heart in a new way. Since that pivotal worship experience in my room, I have enjoyed God's manifest presence in praise and worship many times. I have also experienced the glory of His presence while studying His precious Word, observing communion and fellowshipping with other believers.

Worshiping God has many facets of reality, as we shall discuss, that make it a central theme of the Scriptures. Understanding true spiritual worship is imperative for all believers who sincerely want to know God more intimately.

☙ *Worship Defined*

As we learn about different aspects of worship, our definition of worship will become more comprehensive. But we can begin with a simple working definition from Webster's Dictionary: "showing honor or reverence to a divine being or supernatural power; to regard with great, even extravagant respect, honor or devotion; to take part in an act of worship."

The Old English spelling of the word is worthship, which aptly conveys the idea that the one to whom we show honor has worth. Worship is not an arrogant demand of God toward His creatures; it is rather a natural response from hearts that comprehend the infinite "worthship" of God—hearts that are surrendered, silent, repentant and mature.

Surrendered heart. The biblical pattern of worship is based on the surrender of the heart to the lordship of Christ. Without the heart reality of obedience and submission to the Word of God, we will never experience true worship in spirit and truth. Participation in the sacraments as well as in charismatic expressions of worship must reflect a heart that is bowed in gratitude and love for God in order to become true expressions of worship.

This is the fundamental essence of worship: I bow my heart before God almighty and acknowledge His supreme lordship over my life. It is realized through total surrender of the worshiper to the One worshiped. Only as we choose to acknowledge God in all our ways (SEE PROV. 3:6) and give Him control of our lives and destinies can we become true worshippers of God.

Silent heart. Worship will not always constitute the forming of words or phrases to utter before God. But it will always involve the humble prostration of our souls before God as we revere His greatness in silence and stillness. The psalmist understood this when he wrote of the Lord, "Be still, and know that I am God" (PS. 46:10, NKJV).

Even in human love, affection is not always expressed verbally. Sometimes more is said through eye contact than could ever be expressed in words. Worship involves "eye contact" with God; it is staring at God! A worshiping heart longs to gaze upon the Beloved and know the fulfillment that comes when that gaze is returned.

Repentant heart. Brokenness over our own sin characterizes a worshiping heart. When Mary came into the Pharisee's house to express her love for Jesus, she wept, washed His feet with her tears and anointed them with a costly ointment. The Pharisee condemned her as a sinner and accused Jesus for not knowing what kind of woman she was. But Jesus rebuked the Pharisee for not offering to wash His feet, the customary thing for a host to do. Then He forgave this sinful woman for all her sins (SEE LUKE 7:36–50).

Mary's tears were an outward manifestation of a heart that was deeply stirred before her Lord. She was repentant and so overcome with desire to express her love that she rejected the protocol of the day and barged into a private home uninvited.

This was not a show. Her tears and her kisses were a sincere expression of her penitent heart.

Mature heart. As we grow in our relationship with God, we will grow in our desire and our ability to worship. Spiritual maturity does not exempt one from being a worshiper; it enables one to worship more perfectly and to teach others to worship.

We were made for worship! God created us with a longing to be rightly related to Him in a loving relationship that evokes worship.

Surrender to His lordship in every area of our lives releases us into greater dimensions of worship that bring new revelation of God to our hearts. With each new revelation, we become more satisfied and walk more fully into the divine destiny for which we were created. The priority of worship God purposed will become the dynamic of our lives that brings true fulfillment. ✾

Fuchsia Pickett is the author of numerous books, including Worship Him *(Charisma House), from which this article is adapted. She has earned doctorates in both theology and divinity and teaches at churches and conferences throughout the United States.*

FOR FURTHER STUDY ON THIS TOPIC:

WORSHIP HIS MAJESTY
BY JACK HAYFORD (REGAL)

A SEEKING HEART
BY ALICIA WILLIAMSON AND SARAH GROVES (NEW HOPE)

THE SATISFIED HEART
BY CAROL NOE (CREATION HOUSE PRESS)

MARIA WOODWORTH-ETTER
by Joseph W. Martin

FORERUNNERS OF FAITH
Pentecostal Evangelist

Maria Beulah Woodworth-Etter was born on July 22, 1844, in a farm home near Lisbon, Ohio. She received very little religious training while growing up, and her father's death in 1855 cut short her academic education. At the age of 11, Maria had to leave home with her older sisters to find work.

In 1857, when she was 13, Maria was gloriously saved and baptized. From the moment of her conversion, she began to sense the call of God on her life.

The Lord began dealing with her about going out into the world and winning the lost. At this time, women preachers were rare, and generally the church did not support women in pulpit ministry. As a result, Maria felt extremely isolated and inadequate to carry out her calling.

Soon after the Civil War ended, Maria married a war veteran who had no interest in the things of God. Everything they set out to do as a couple met with failure.

Maria busied herself with raising a family, but the call of God persisted. In fact, the more she resisted it, the more intensely it gripped her.

One day Maria had a vision in which she saw an open Bible. The Lord said to her "Go, and I will be with you." Finally, after losing five of her six children to death, Maria surrendered her life fully and totally to God. In 1880 she stepped out in faith, and against all odds and tradition, she decided to conduct a series of meetings at a home in her community.

At the first meeting, Maria got up and read the Scripture twice that was to be the foundation for her teaching. The power of God came upon her, and she preached for the next hour and a quarter.

People everywhere began to weep—and by the time the series of meetings had ended, more than 20 people had been saved.

Maria quickly became well-known. Her successful evangelistic meetings often made front-page news and proved to many people that God could use a woman to preach the gospel.

For the next 44 years Maria Woodworth-Etter conducted hundreds of meetings all over the country. Attendance in her services reached 25,000. The power of God would flow mightily, manifesting miracles, healings, and other signs and wonders, as well as numerous conversions. Her ministry spanned both the Holiness and the early Pentecostal eras, and she was instrumental in spreading the teaching of both movements.

Maria died in Indianapolis, Indiana, in 1924, after establishing a local church—still in existence today—that she pastored for six years. 🏵

Joseph Martin is a Pentecostal historian-researcher and is the Resource Director at Victory Bible Institute in Tulsa, Oklahoma. He has compiled The Spirit-Filled Woman *devotional (Charisma House) along with several other books.*

Lord, Give Us New Hearts

by Juanita Bynum

It's time to seek the Lord AS never before. As we do, our consecration and devotion will intensify, and we will become remarkably more like Him.

Right before we held our conference in Chicago in 2000, God began to get my attention on the subject of the new heart. We were planning to have the event in a beautiful church that seats 4,500 people; it was going to be impressive.

But a few days before the conference, we ran into difficulties and had to switch to another facility. This one was not as big and was more difficult for the people to get to.

I found myself going into turmoil. How could this happen? We had been fasting and praying for this meeting!

God began showing me that my burden was not for the people and what I felt they would receive. I was more concerned about my image and what I would project.

As the tears rolled down my face, God said: "Jesus made Himself of no reputation...yet it is your reputation that has become most important to you. You are thinking about all you are doing, the major platforms where you are able to speak and all the exposure you are getting. But what is the condition of your heart toward Me and toward My people?"

Confused, I said to the Lord, "My heart? You know that every-thing I am doing, I am doing to please You."

God said: "You have been working under the assumption that all your works have impressed Me, and I am not impressed by any of it. I want to give you a new heart."

"A new heart?" I asked. "But I already feel like I am saved."

"Your salvation is according to the salvation of the traditional church," He responded. "Now I want to save you for real."

❧ *The True Heart Revealed*

Years before, I had accepted Christ as my personal Savior. At that time, my spirit man was converted, and I began to get into the Word. I wanted to transform my mind so that my life could begin to experience what had happened in my heart.

But somewhere along the line, I had started reading the Word of God to prepare me to preach—not to convert my own mind. My ministry became my career, and even though I knew I had been called to preach, I believe it was God's compassion for His people that kept me there.

When I had told God I was willing to go, and a cry for help rose up from His people, He anointed me and used me in His work. Yet He loved me so much that He said, "While you are preaching to others, I do not want to forget about you." He wanted to continue teaching me while I was teaching others.

In speaking to me about my heart, the Lord took me to Jeremiah 17:9-10: "The heart is deceitful above all things, and it is exceedingly perverse and corrupt and severely, mortally sick! Who can know it [perceive, understand, be acquainted with his own heart and mind]? I the Lord search the mind, I try the heart, even to give to every man according to his ways, according to the fruit of his doings" *(THE AMPLIFIED BIBLE)*.

As I meditated on this verse, I had to be honest with myself; my heart was not right. I had to ask, "Am I really saved? Does Jesus really live here? Am I sure, beyond the shadow of a doubt, that He lives in me? I do not have any doubt that He uses me...but does Jesus live here? Am I His?"

God began to minister to me. He took me to John 10:26: "But you do not believe and trust and rely on Me, because you do not belong to My fold—you are no sheep of Mine."

This is the message God gave me: Sin and God cannot dwell in the same heart at the same time. Righteousness and unrighteousness cannot dwell in the same temple.

In order to be transformed, we must renew our minds every day. When the renewed mind lines up with the conversion that is in our hearts, we are new creatures—completely, inside and out. We must choose whether to follow the stubborn habits stored in our memories or to submit to the wisdom that flows out of our new hearts.

If you are seeking God, you already know that we are entering a new era. It is time to fall down at the altar and ask God to renew our hearts. It is time to become more like Jesus—for real.

⅋ *The Impossible Dream*

God has brought me into relationships with a few people who, although they are not saved, were raised in the church. One of them said to me:"If somebody in Christendom can find a way to make living for God attainable and reachable, then you do not know how many people would come to Christ."

When this gentleman suggested to me that people were looking for a God who was attainable and reachable, I asked in my heart,"Is God attainable?"I realized I could not answer that question.

I was forced to turn and look within myself. Through the years I had struggled with feelings of spiritual inadequacy.

I looked at the many people God had placed in my life as spiritual examples. I felt as if I could never be like them because they were the epitome of spiritual perfection.

Once I started my own ministry, God helped me realize the error of my heart. I discovered that other people had the same feelings about me. They would say to me:"Prophetess Bynum, you have really blessed my life. You are such a woman of God."

The truth is that during that time God was breaking me and breaking things off me. But in the eyes of other people, I appeared to be perfect. The image of who I was as a woman of God had become unattainable. But the image in their minds was not reality.

We have to be real with people. If we consistently paint a picture that everything is perfect, as if to say,"You know you have reached God when you look like me, dress like me, walk and talk like me,"then we have totally missed God!

❧ The Heart vs. the Mind

We are all struggling in our own way, trying to make sure that we do what is right from our hearts. But I've discovered that we function mainly out of our intellects.

The brain teaches us to scheme, lie and manipulate. But God has put a spirit of conviction in our hearts that corrects us when we do something wrong.

The world has trained us to bypass our hearts' conviction and to operate within the realm of our minds and emotions. This is why no one is seeking after God for a changed heart. We do not want to change; we want only to feel better—for the moment.

The Bible says that we are born with a nature that has great potential to do wrong. When we come into the world, our hearts are already shaped for iniquity and sin (SEE PS. 51:5).

When you look at our society, you see that this is true—and I am not just talking about the secular world. We are in church, dancing and shouting and speaking in tongues, yet we have hearts of iniquity just as the world does.

It has taken the fear of ongoing terrorist attacks from another country to bring us to our knees. It took this incident to help us realize that in spite of everything we have, we need the Lord.

When we walk with hearts that are born into sin, seeking the Lord is not important to us. Our hearts do not come with a "Yes, Lord" in them. They must be changed. But how?

❧ Our First Priority

You cannot walk in God's ways unless you fear Him as God and submit to Him, totally and completely. Above this, you cannot walk in His ways unless you love Him from the center of your being—your heart.

❧ Loving

God brings about a commitment to Him, as well as a change of character. So if you say, "I love You, Lord," but still walk in your own ways, then you do not really love the Lord.

You can appreciate Him for the life and breath He has given you.

You are grateful when He makes a way for you out of no way and for all the things He permits you to have. But that is materialism. It cannot become real love until you become committed and submitted to His ways.

Beware of the deception that can come with the prosperity of God's blessing upon your life. Just as God needed to humble the Israelites and create a spiritual hunger within them, so He has humbled us and allowed us to hunger after Him *(SEE DEUT. 8:2-3)*.

Today God's people must ask for new hearts. The problem is finding those who are willing to say: "I have to have the heart of God. I have to have a new heart. I have to have a real relationship with God outside the pews, outside the choir roll, outside my favorite preacher or evangelist."

Without all the props and all the drama, where does your relationship start? What is the real purpose of your relationship with God?

Having taken a deep look at the church, I have to ask this question: How can the church do the work of the Spirit to the point that it has the power to be as compassionate as Christ Himself? Where will we find the eternal love we need to embrace the kinds of sinners who are coming to Christ in this hour?

ﾟ *Prayer Is Key*

It's time to take the keys of God's Word, and from the deep chambers of our hearts, unshackle our minds—and ultimately the world—from the enemy's bondage. Prayer is our vital connection to God through the vehicle of our new hearts.

Here are a few Scriptures to get you started as you seek God in prayer daily. Put yourself in these Scriptures as you meditate on the Word.

Prayer Keys for the Heart. "Create in me a clean heart, O God, and renew a right, persevering, and steadfast spirit within me" *(Ps. 51:10).*

"A new heart will I give you and a new spirit will I put within you, and I will take away the stony heart out of your flesh and give you a heart of flesh" *(EZEK. 36:26).*

"Search me [thoroughly], O God, and know my heart! Try me and know my thoughts! And see if there is any wicked or hurtful way in me, and lead me in the way everlasting" *(Ps. 139:23-24).*

Prayer Keys for the Mind. "For who has known or understood the mind (counsels and purposes) of the Lord so as to guide and instruct Him and give Him knowledge? But we have the mind of Christ (the Messiah) and do hold the thoughts (feelings and purposes) of His heart" *(1 Cor. 2:16).*

"And be constantly renewed in the spirit of your mind [having a fresh mental and spiritual attitude], and put on the new nature (the regenerate self) created in God's image [Godlike] in true righteousness and holiness" *(Eph. 4:23-24).*

"You will guard him and keep him in perfect and constant peace whose mind [both its inclination and its character] is stayed on You, because he commits himself to You, leans on You, and hopes confidently in You" *(Is. 26:3).*

I have a mandate to preach the "new heart" message because so many believers are deceived (as I was). If you're one of them, you need to ask God to give you a new heart. It is time to return to the Lord. Nothing is more important than the matters of the heart. ✿

Juanita Bynum is the author of Matters of the Heart, *published by Charisma House, from which this article is adapted.*

FOR FURTHER STUDY ON THIS TOPIC:

MATTERS OF THE HEART
BY JUANITA BYNUM (CHARISMA HOUSE)

TRIUMPHS OF THE HEART
BY CHERYL FORD (CROSSWAY BOOKS)

A HEART LIKE HIS
BY BETH MOORE (BROADMAN & HOLMAN)

LORD, TEACH US YOUR WAYS

by Francis Frangipane

Our desire must be to know God as Moses did, not just in His mighty acts, but in the intentions of His heart.

Mount Horeb, where first Moses and later the prophet Elijah sought refuge during times of persecution in their lives, was not what it appeared to be. Though forbidding and barren, as the name "Horeb" ("desolation") implies, it actually came to symbolize that season in a person's life during which a desolate soul could find the presence of God. Both Elijah and Moses before him found fresh encounters with God on Horeb. Surrounded by the bleak and barren environment, the Lord reduced His servants to one focus: God alone.

The Horeb experience tells us that God accommodates our times of desolation and uses them to prepare us for greater glory. Out of our barrenness comes a renewed dependency upon God, from which new assignments and increased power emerge.

It was in the cleft of a rock near Horeb that Moses prayed, "If I have found grace in Your sight, show me now Your way, that I may know You" *(Ex. 33:13, NKJV).*

And it was here that the Lord, in turn, promised, "My presence will go with you, and I will give you rest" *(v. 14).*

We cannot say we truly know God if we remain ignorant of His ways. To know the ways of a person is to know his heart's motivations as well as how he would respond to the blessings and challenges of life. Moses knew the Lord in the deepest intimacy possible; he knew God's ways.

The Bible tells us that the Lord revealed His acts to the sons of Israel, but He made known His ways to Moses *(Ps. 103:7).* To know the ways of God is to know the motives of His heart and the secrets of His passions. It is to be amazed at the resolve of His love and compelled to humility by His attraction to the lowly.

The Lord had promised Moses, "My presence will go with you." When God's presence accompanies our actions, all the energy we once spent worrying and planning is reclaimed and offered back to God in praise and effective service.

The outcome of being companioned through life with Christ is in His next promise, "I will give you rest" *(Ex. 33:14)*. To enter God's rest does not imply that we have become inactive but that God has become active. Thus, Jesus calls, "Come to Me, all you who labor and are heavy laden, and I will give you rest" *(Matt. 11:28)*.

How the church today, weary and desperate, needs to return to Jesus and re-enter God's rest! When we are yoked to Christ, our burdens are transferred to the vastness of His strength and abilities. He becomes to us an untiring resource for our weakness; He is unfailing wisdom for our ignorance.

At the place of rest, Christ becomes a continual life-spring of grace and virtue. We can cease from our anxious labors and, unfettered from our ideas and traditions, serve Him in the unlimited strength of His might.

God has always been more concerned with the condition of our hearts than with the activity of our hands. What we become to Him is far more consequential than all we shall ever do for Him. He wants our love and companionship.

Indeed, the Scriptures tell us that He "jealously desires the Spirit which He has made to dwell in us" *(James 4:5, NASB)*. Thus, if our devotion to our task exceeds our devotion to Him, He will personally hinder our success. It is out of love that God delivers us from the unanointed momentum of our zeal. He intentionally dries up our vigor.

The Lord insists that our success originate not from our strength but from our union with Him. Our time of desolation, brokenness and disappointment becomes a tool in His hand by which He works within us a deeper dependency upon His strength.

Alone with God on Horeb, Moses prayed, "Show me Your glory" *(Ex. 33:18, NKJV)*. The Lord responded, "I will make all My goodness pass before you" *(v. 19)*. At the center of Christ's resplendent glory is His incomparable goodness. Indeed, our Horeb experience becomes the very site where, in spite of our sense of failure, God reveals to us His goodness.

To be personally restored to the knowledge of God's goodness is what Elijah desperately needed. So it is for us.

☙ *The Cave of Withdrawal*

It can be a crushing experience to give your very best and still fall short. Elijah had been discouraged with his inability to effect revival in God's people. He fled Jezebel and traveled south nearly 200 miles to Horeb, where he lodged in a cave on the mountain side.

Scripture tells us that "hope deferred makes the heart sick" (PROV. 13:12). Elijah had lost hope that revival would come to Israel. When we lose hope we simultaneously lose faith, for faith is the substance of the thing hoped for. Without hope or faith, all we have is empty religion.

When we become heartsick with disappointment and discouragement, we also lose perspective. We feel that we are responsible for the results. We must remember that, apart from the cooperating work of the Holy Spirit, no man can change another person's heart, much less the heart of a city or nation.

Much of Elijah's discouragement came from the false expectations he had placed upon himself. Often when we receive an assignment from the Lord, we, like Elijah, begin immediately to imagine the results. We project ourselves prematurely into a place of success and fulfillment.

Yet we do not know what the result will be—only that we should obey the Lord. We must leave the fulfillment in the hands of Him who does "exceedingly abundantly above all that we ask or think" (EPH. 3:20).

Elijah withdrew into a cave on Horeb. For us, self-pity can become a spiritual cave. It can trap us in a dark hole of loneliness and pain. In this place of isolation we fail to hear the encouragement of God; all we hear is the echo of our own voices magnifying and distorting our problems.

Elijah was alone and despairing, yet the Lord knew his heart. "What are you doing here?" the Lord asked him (1 KIN. 19:9).

And Elijah said, "I have been very zealous for the Lord God of hosts; for the children of Israel have forsaken Your covenant, torn down Your altars, and killed Your prophets with the sword. I alone am left; and they seek to take my life" *(v. 10)*.

Elijah wanted desperately to see the nation awakened, but he did not understand the role God would have him play. Perhaps Elijah's main mistake was that he was personally shouldering the burden of Israel's revival. Not knowing his own place, he assumed the place of God.

Calling Elijah out of the cave, the Lord told him, "Go out, and stand on the mountain before the Lord" *(v. 11)*. As Elijah stepped out of the cave's darkness, an awesome event occurred.

"And behold, the Lord passed by, and a great and strong wind tore into the mountains and broke the rocks in pieces before the Lord, but the Lord was not in the wind; and after the wind an earthquake, but the Lord was not in the earthquake; and after the earthquake a fire, but the Lord was not in the fire; and after the fire a still small voice" *(vv. 11-12)*.

🐦 *A New Revelation of God*

There are times when, to lead us on into new authority and blessings, God must liberate us from the container of our previous experiences. The Lord was passing by, but He was not in the wind, the earthquake or the fire, all of which were familiar symbols to Elijah. The Lord who caused these mighty manifestations was not in them.

For Elijah, mighty manifestations had been signs of God's approval. But something new was at hand that required a fresh submission to the living God. A double portion of power was coming! The distinguishing characteristic of this new anointing would be seen not only in supernatural manifestations but also in greater wisdom and compassion.

Earthquakes, fires and storms—the signs that accompanied Elijah—are the signs of our times as well. But to enter the double portion, we must learn to recognize God's nearness when there are no "earthquakes" or "storms" to capture our attention. He demands we enter a more refined relationship with Him, one that is based on His love and the whisper of His word, not merely upon spiritual phenomena or the issues of our times.

After the last sign, there came "a still small voice" *(1 KIN. 19:12)*. Elijah recognized it: The presence of God was returning. Elijah "wrapped his face in his mantle" lest he look upon God *(v. 13)*.

Perhaps it was near this very site that Moses, 500 years earlier, hid when the Lord passed by. Now it was Elijah's turn. Entering this eternal stillness was the person of God.

We too must learn to hear the voice of Him who rarely speaks audibly and observe the actions of Him who is otherwise invisible. Elijah would gain the courage to endure Jezebel's wrath the same way Moses faced the rage of Pharaoh: "He endured, as seeing Him who is invisible" *(HEB. 11:27)*. We must learn to detect, without great signs, the still, small voice of God.

He will not fight for our attention; He must be sought. He will not startle us; He must be perceived. It took no special skill to "discern" the earthquake, the fire or the great storm. But to sense the holy quiet of God, our other activities must cease.

In our world of great pressures and continual distractions, the attention of our hearts must rise to the invisible world of God's Spirit. We must learn to see Him who is unseen.

☙ *A New Beginning*

In the quieting of Elijah's heart, the Lord in His goodness drew near, reassuring Elijah that he was not alone in his battle: There were still 7,000 Israelites who had not bowed to Baal. Next, a new commission came.

The Lord told Elijah to anoint Hazael as king over Syria and Jehu as king over Israel. He also was to train Elisha, who would be his successor *(1 KIN. 19:15-16)*.

At Horeb, God released a "double portion" of spiritual power. Although the Lord gave the new anointing to Elijah, it would be Elisha who would walk in it *(2 KIN. 2:9-14)*. Elisha would do twice as many miracles. More than any other Old Testament prophet, Elisha's works would most resemble those of Christ Himself.

Elijah did not personally bring national restoration, but he prepared the way for Elisha, who brought the closest thing to revival the northern tribes ever experienced. Out of his Horeb encounter with God, Elijah received a greater understanding of his place in God. His call was not to establish, but to "go before" and prepare the way for greater things to come.

In fact, Elijah was so successful at "preparing the way" that his spiritual anointing was apportioned to John the Baptist as a herald to Christ's first coming.

Elijah is destined to prepare the way for Christ's second coming as well (SEE MAL. 4:5-6; MATT. 17:11).

As this age ends, God's promise to us is that we too shall receive a "double portion" (IS. 61:7; JOHN 14:12). What can this mean but that the Lord is going to reveal Himself to us in glories we have never known before?

Do not despair if you find yourself in a time of desolation. In truth, with God, our desolation is but preparation for a new beginning of power and service—an opportunity for God to "show us His ways."

Our task is to be still and know that Christ is God. He shall triumph over all His foes. He will be exalted in all the earth, and in Him is the stronghold of God.

O Master, how easily I fall into dead religious habits and spiritual dullness! Lord, I long to know Your ways, to have eyes that really see and ears that clearly hear. Teach me, Lord Jesus, the intimacies of God. Remove the mystery surrounding Yourself that I might truly know You. Forgive me for looking for signs instead of listening for Your voice. O God, how I long to truly know You as Moses did, to abide in Your glory. Restore to Your church the double portion You have promised, and guide us into the fullness of Your power. In Jesus' name. Amen. ✿

Francis Frangipane is the pastor of River of Life Ministries, Cedar Rapids, Iowa, and the author of The Three Battlegrounds, The House of the Lord *and five other books. He is also a contributor to* Charisma *magazine.*

FOR FURTHER STUDY ON THIS TOPIC:

THE STRONGHOLD OF GOD
BY FRANCIS FRANGIPANE (CHARISMA HOUSE)

THE GOD OF ALL COMFORT
BY HANNAH WHITALL SMITH (MOODY)

KNOWING GOD
BY J.I. PACKER (INTERVARSITY PRESS)

EXALT GOD ABOVE ALL

by A.W. Tozer

Many of us claim that God is first in our lives. But do we live out this reality in our everyday existence—or have we made something else preeminent?

Order, both in nature and in human life, depends upon right relationships; to achieve harmony each thing must be in its proper position relative to each other thing. That's why it is so essential for God to have His proper place in our lives. When He does not, everything is out of order.

We are right when, and only when, we stand in a right position relative to God, and we are wrong so far and so long as we stand in any other position.

So let us begin with God. Back of all, above all, before all is God; first in sequential order, above in rank and station, exalted in dignity and honor. As the self-existent One He gave being to all things, and all things exist out of Him and for Him. "Thou art worthy, O Lord, to receive glory and honour and power: for Thou hast created all things, and for Thy pleasure they are and were created" (REV. 4:11, KJV).

Every soul belongs to God and exists by His pleasure. God being who and what He is, and we being who and what we are, the only thinkable relation between us is one of full lordship on His part and complete submission on ours. We owe Him every honor that is in our power to give Him. Our everlasting grief lies in giving Him anything less.

The pursuit of God will embrace the labor of bringing our total personality into conformity to His. I do not here refer to the act of justification by faith in Christ. I speak of a voluntary exalting of God to His proper station over us and a willing surrender of our whole being to the place of worshipful submission that the Creator creature circumstance makes proper.

The moment we make up our minds that we are going on with this determination to exalt God over all, we step out of the world's parade. We shall find ourselves out of adjustment to the ways of the world and increasingly so as we make progress in the holy way. We shall acquire a new viewpoint; a new psychology will be formed within us; a new power will begin to surprise us by its upsurgings and its outgoings.

Our break with the world will be the direct outcome of our changed relation to God. For the world of fallen men does not honor God. Millions call themselves by His name, it is true, and pay some token respect to Him, but a simple test will show how little He is really honored among them.

Let the average man be put to the proof on the question of who or what is above, and his true position will be exposed. Let him be forced into making a choice between God and money, between God and man, between God and personal ambition, God and self, God and human love, and God will take second place every time. Those other things will be exalted above. However the man may protest, the proof is in the choices he makes day after day throughout his life.

"Be exalted, O Lord" *(Ps. 21:13, NKJV)* is the language of victorious spiritual experience. It is a little key to unlock the door to great treasures of grace. It is central in the life of God in the soul.

Let the seeking man reach a place where life and lips join to say continually "Be exalted, O Lord," and a thousand minor problems will be solved at once. His Christian life ceases to be the complicated thing it had been before and becomes the very essence of simplicity. By the exercise of his will he has set his course, and on that course he will stay as if guided by an automatic pilot.

Let no one imagine that he will lose anything of human dignity by this voluntary sell-out of his all to God. His deep disgrace lay in his unnatural usurpation of the place of God. His honor will be proved by restoring again that stolen throne. In exalting God over all he finds his own highest honor upheld.

Anyone who might feel reluctant to surrender his will to the will of another should remember Jesus' words, "Whoever commits sin is a slave of sin" *(JOHN 8:34)*. We must of necessity be servant to someone, either to God or to sin.

The sinner prides himself on his independence, completely overlooking the fact that he is the weak slave of the sins that rule his members. The man who surrenders to Christ exchanges a cruel slave driver for a kind and gentle Master whose yoke is easy and whose burden is light.

I hope it is clear that there is a logic behind God's claim to preeminence. That place is His by every right in earth or heaven. While we take to ourselves the place that is His, the whole course of our lives is out of joint. Nothing will or can restore order till our hearts make the great decision: God shall be exalted above.

"Those who honor Me I will honor" (1 Sam. 2:30), God said once to a priest of Israel, and that ancient law of the kingdom stands today unchanged by the passing of time or the changes of dispensation. The whole Bible and every page of history proclaim the perpetuation of that law.

"If anyone serves Me, him My Father will honor," (John 12:26), Jesus said, tying in the old with the new and revealing the essential unity of His ways with men.

Sometimes the best way to see a thing is to look at its opposite. Eli and his sons are placed in the priesthood with the stipulation that they honor God in their lives and ministrations. They fail to do this, and God sends Samuel to announce the consequences.

Unknown to Eli, this law of reciprocal honor has been all the while secretly working, and now the time has come for judgment to fall. Hophni and Phineas, the degenerate priests, fall in battle; the wife of Hophni dies in childbirth; Israel flees before her enemies; the ark of God is captured by the Philistines; and the old man Eli falls backward and dies of a broken neck. Thus stark, utter tragedy followed upon Eli's failure to honor God.

Now over against this set almost any Bible character who honestly tried to glorify God in his earthly walk. See how God winked at weakness and overlooked failures as He poured upon His servants grace and blessing untold. Let it be Abraham, Jacob, David, Daniel, Elijah or whom you will; honor followed honor as harvest the seed.

The man of God set his heart to exalt God above all; God

accepted his intention as fact and acted accordingly. Not perfection, but holy intention made the difference.

In our Lord Jesus Christ this law was seen in simple perfection. In His lowly manhood He humbled Himself and gladly gave all glory to His Father in heaven. He sought not His own honor but the honor of God who sent Him.

"If I honor Myself," He said on one occasion, "My honor is nothing. It is My Father who honors Me" *(JOHN 8:54)*. So far had the Pharisees departed from this law that they could not understand one who honored God at his own expense. "I honor My Father," Jesus said to them, "and you dishonor Me" *(v. 49)*.

Another saying of Jesus, and a most disturbing one, was put in the form of a question. "How can you believe, who receive honor from one another, and do not seek the honor that comes from the only God?" *(JOHN 5:44)*. If I understand this correctly, Christ taught here the alarming doctrine that the desire for honor among men made belief impossible.

Is this sin at the root of religious unbelief? I believe it may be. The whole course of life is upset by failure to put God where He belongs. We exalt ourselves instead of God, and the curse follows.

In our desire after God let us keep always in mind that God also has desire, and His desire is toward the sons of men, and more particularly toward those sons of men who will make the once-for-all decision to exalt Him over all. Such as these are precious to God above all treasures of earth or sea.

In them God finds a theater where He can display His exceeding kindness toward us in Christ Jesus. With them God can walk unhindered; toward them He can act like the God He is.

In speaking thus I have one fear: that I may convince the mind before God can win the heart. For this God-above-all position is one not easy to take. The mind may approve it while not having the consent of the will to put it into effect.

Though the imagination races ahead to honor God, the will may lag behind, and the man must make the decision before the heart can know any real satisfaction. God wants the whole person, and He will not rest till He gets us in entirety.

Let us pray over this in detail, throwing ourselves at God's feet and meaning everything we say. Let's ask God today to be exalted over our possessions, our friendships, our comforts, our reputations. Let's ask Him to take His proper place of honor above our ambitions, our likes and dislikes, our family, our health and even life itself.

No one who prays thus in sincerity need wait long for tokens of divine acceptance. God will unveil His glory before His servant's eyes, and He will place all His treasures at the disposal of such a one, for He knows that His honor is safe in consecrated hands. ❀

 A.W. Tozer (1897-1963) was pastor of Southside Alliance Church in Chicago for 31 years. He also was the author of more than 40 books, including Faith Beyond Reason; Man: The Dwelling Place of God *and* The Knowledge of the Holy.

FOR FURTHER STUDY ON THIS TOPIC:

THE GOD CATCHERS
BY TOMMY TENNEY (THOMAS NELSON)

THE WAYS OF GOD
BY HENRY T. BLACKABY (BROADMAN AND HOLMAN)

REACHING FOR THE INVISIBLE GOD
BY PHILIP YANCEY (ZONDERVAN)

AMANDA BERRY SMITH
by Joseph W. Martin

FORERUNNERS OF FAITH
Missionary Evangelist

Amanda Berry Smith was born a slave in Maryland on January 23, 1837, the oldest of 13 children. Her father purchased the family's freedom when Amanda was in her early teens and moved the family to York County, Pennsylvania.

Amanda had very little formal education. At a young age, she began doing domestic housework as a means of support. Her mother died when she was 14.

Amanda married in 1854, but her husband died while serving in an African American military unit in the Civil War. In 1855 she had her first spiritual experience. During a serious illness, she fell into a trance and had a vision of an angel telling her: "Go back, go back, go back."

Then Amanda saw herself preaching before thousands of people with great demonstrations of power. The vision lasted for about two hours. When she came out of the trance, the illness was gone, and she recovered miraculously. Amanda was converted when she was 19.

In 1863 Amanda remarried but after only a few years was widowed again. In 1868 she had a spiritual experience she called "entire satisfaction," during which she devoted herself entirely to the Lord. This led her to begin doing evangelistic work in New York City. She had a gift for speaking and singing and became known as "The Singing Pilgrim."

Amanda attended many "holiness" camp meetings where she was asked to preach and sing. She received inspiration at the African Methodist Episcopal Church (AME) but could not be ordained in that denomination because she was a woman.

Still, the call of God was evident, so she gave up domestic work and pursued the life of an itinerant evangelist. One of the most significant characteristics of her ministry was her tremendous prayer life and consecration to God.

From 1870-78, Amanda traveled all over the United States. For the next 13 years, she ministered abroad, establishing churches in Liberia and West Africa. Her meetings were marked by tremendous power that attracted large audiences.

Once in India, a mob disrupted her outdoor meeting. Amanda immediately got down and cried out to God. Soon a holy stillness came over the audience, and she had their undivided attention.

In 1892, Amanda returned to the United States, settling in the Chicago, Illinois, area. Later she established the first orphanage in Illinois for African American children. In 1912 she retired to Florida, where she died three years later—the most outstanding female evangelist of her era. ❀

Joseph Martin is a Pentecostal historian-researcher and is the Resource Director at Victory Bible Institute in Tulsa, Oklahoma. He has compiled The Spirit-Filled Woman *devotional (Creation House) along with several other books.*

BECOMING ONE WITH GOD
by Hannah Whitall Smith

God's goal for every believer is oneness with him. To reach it, we must take on the character of Christ.

All the dealings God has with the soul of the believer are to bring it into oneness with Himself, that the final prayer Jesus prayed before He died may be fulfilled: "That they all may be one, as You, Father, are in Me, and I in You; that they also may be one in Us....I in them, and You in Me; that they may be made perfect in one, and that the world may know that You have sent Me, and have loved them as You have loved Me" *(JOHN 17:21-23, NKJV).*

This divine union was the glorious purpose in the heart of God for His people before the foundation of the world. It was accomplished in the death of Christ. It has been made known by the Scriptures. It is realized as an actual experience by many of God's dear children.

However, it is not experienced by all. God has not hidden this union or made it hard, but the eyes of many are too dim and their hearts too unbelieving for them to grasp it. It is for the purpose of bringing His people into the personal and actual realization of this that the Lord calls upon them so earnestly and so repeatedly to abandon themselves to Him. Thus He may work in them all the good pleasure of His will.

All the previous steps in the Christian life lead up to this. The Lord has made us for it, and until we have understood it and voluntarily consented to embrace it, the "travail of His soul" *(Is. 53:11, KJV)* for us is not satisfied, nor have our hearts found their destined and real rest.

☙ *Reality of the Christlife*

The usual course of Christian experience is pictured in the history of the disciples. First, they were awakened to see their condition and their need and came to Christ and gave their allegiance to Him. Then they followed Him, worked for Him and believed in Him.

Yet how unlike Him they were, seeking to be set up one above the other! They ran away from the cross, misunderstanding His mission and His words. They forsook their Lord in time of danger. But still they were sent out to preach, recognized by Him as His disciples, possessing power to work for Him. They knew Christ as their Lord and Master but did not yet know Him as their life.

Then came Pentecost, and these same disciples came to know Him as one with them in actual union, their very indwelling life. From then on they knew what He was within them, working in them to will and to do of His good pleasure, delivering them by the law of the Spirit of His life, from the bondage to the law of sin and death under which they had been held.

No longer did their wills and interests war with His. His will alone motivated them. His interest alone was dear to them. They were made one with Him.

Surely all can recognize this picture, though perhaps the final stage of it has not yet been fully reached. You may have given up much to follow Christ. You may have believed on Him and worked for Him and loved Him—and yet may not be like Him.

Allegiance you know, and confidence you know, but you do not yet know union. There are two wills, two interests, two lives. You have not yet lost your own life that you may live only in His.

Once it was "I and not Christ." Next it was "I and Christ." Perhaps now it is even "Christ and I." But has it yet come to be Christ only, and not I at all?

If you have followed me to this point, you will surely now be ready to take the definite step of faith which will lead your soul out of self and into Christ. You will then be prepared to abide in Him forever and to know no life but His. You need only to understand what the Scriptures teach about this marvelous union and see that it is intended for you.

Read 1 Corinthians 3:16: "Do you not know you are the temple of God and that the Spirit of God dwells in you?" *(NKJV)*, and then look at the opening of the chapter to see whom Paul was addressing—"babes in Christ"who were"yet carnal"and walked according to men *(1 COR. 3:1).* You will then see that this soul-union of which I speak, this unspeakably glorious mystery of an indwelling God, is the possession of even the weakest and most failing believer in Christ. It is true that every believer's"body is the temple of the Holy Spirit who is in you, whom you have from God" *(1 COR. 6:19).*

But although this is true, it is also equally true that the believer has to know it and live in the power of it. Like the treasures under a man's field which existed there before they were known or used by him, so does the life of Christ dwell in each believer before he knows it and lives in it. Its power is not manifested until, intelligently and voluntarily, the believer ceases from his own life and accepts Christ's life in its place.

But it is very important not to make any mistakes here. This union with Christ is not a matter of emotions but of character. It is not something we are to feel but something we are to be. The vital thing is not the feeling, but the reality.

☞ *Living in our Emotions*

No one can be one with Christ who is not truly Christlike. Yet often strong emotions of love and joy are taken as an indication of divine union in cases where essential proofs of a Christlike life and character are lacking. This is completely contrary to the Scripture declaration that"He who says he abides in Him ought himself also to walk just as He walked" *(1 JOHN 2:6).* Oneness with Christ means being made"partakers of [His] nature" *(2 PET. 1:4).*

If we are really one with Christ, it will not be contrary to our nature to be Christlike and to walk as He walked; it will be in accordance with our nature. Sweetness, gentleness, meekness, patience, long-suffering, charity, and kindness will all be natural to the Christian who is a partaker of the nature of Christ. It could not be otherwise.

But people who live in their emotions do not always see this. They feel so at one with Christ that they look no further than this feeling.

They often delude themselves by thinking they have come into divine union, when all the while their nature and dispositions are still under the sway of self-love.

Our emotions are most untrustworthy and are largely the result of our physical conditions or our natural temperaments. It is a fatal mistake, therefore, to make them the test of our oneness with Christ.

This mistake works both ways. If I have very joyous emotions, I may be deluded into thinking I have entered into the divine union when I have not. If I have no emotions, I may grieve over my failure to enter into the divine union when I really have entered.

Character is the only real test. God is holy, and those who are one with Him will be holy also.

Our Lord Himself expressed His oneness with the Father in these words: "The Son can do nothing of Himself, but what He sees the Father do; for whatever He does, the Son also does in like manner" (JOHN 5:19). The test Christ gave by which the reality of His oneness with the Father was to be known was the fact that He did the works of the Father. I know of no other test for us now.

☞ *Awareness of Christ's Presence*

Having guarded against the danger of an emotional experience of divine union, let us consider how the reality is to be reached. First I would say that it is not a new attitude to be taken by God but only a new attitude to be taken by us.

If we are really children of God, then our hearts are already the temple of God and Christ is already within us. What is needed, therefore, is only that we recognize His presence and yield fully to His control.

Since the day of your conversion the Lord has been dwelling in your heart, but you have lived in ignorance of it. During all that time, every moment might have been passed in the sunshine of His sweet presence and every step taken under His advice. But because you did not know it and did not look for Him there, your life has been lonely and full of failure.

But now that I make you aware of this, how are you going to receive it? Are you glad to have Him? Will you throw every door wide open to welcome Him in? Will you joyfully and thankfully give up your life to Him?

Will you consult Him about everything and let Him decide each step and mark out every path? Will you invite Him into your innermost chambers and share your most hidden life with Him?

Will you say "Yes" to His longing for union with you? Will you, with a glad and eager surrender, hand yourself and all that concerns you over into His hands? If you will do this your soul will begin to know something of the joy of union with Christ.

It seems too wonderful to be true that such poor, weak, foolish beings as we are were created for such an end as this. Yet it is a blessed reality. We are even commanded to enter into it.

We are exhorted to lay down our lives so that His life may be lived in us. We are asked to have no interests but His interests, to share His riches, to enter into His joys, to partake of His sorrows, to have the same mind He had, and to think and feel and act and walk as He did.

Will we agree to all this? The Lord will not force it on us because He wants us as His companions and His friends, and a forced union would be incompatible with this. It must be voluntary on our part. The bride must say a willing "yes" to the bridegroom, or the joy of their union is in question.

Can we say a willing "yes" to our Lord?

It is a very simple yet real transaction. There are three steps. First, we must be convinced that the Scriptures teach this glorious indwelling of God. Then we must surrender our whole selves to Him to be possessed by Him. And finally, we must believe that He has taken possession and is dwelling in us. We must begin to consider ourselves dead and to consider Christ as our only life.

We must maintain this attitude of soul unwaveringly. It will help us to say, "I have been crucified with Christ; it is no longer I who live, but Christ lives in me" (Gal. 2:20) over and over, day and night, until it becomes the habitual breathing of our souls. We must continually deny self and put on the life of Christ.

We must do this not only by faith but also in practice. We must continually put self to death in all the details of daily life and let Christ live and work in us instead. We must never do the selfish thing but always the Christlike thing. We must let this become, by its constant repetition, the attitude of our whole being.

As we do this we will understand at least something of what it means to be made one with Christ as He and the Father are one. Christ left all to be joined to us. We must also leave everything to be joined to Him in this divine union that words cannot express, but for which our Lord prayed when He said, "I do not pray for these alone, but also for those who will believe in Me through their word; that they all may be one, as You, Father, are in Me, and I in You; that they also may be one in Us" *(JOHN 17:20-21).*

Hannah Whitall Smith (1832-1911) was a popular writer and speaker. She and her husband, Robert Pearsall Smith, participated in holiness meetings in the United States and in England, where they laid the groundwork for the famous Keswick conferences.

FOR FURTHER STUDY ON THIS TOPIC:

THE GOD OF ALL COMFORT
BY HANNAH WHITALL SMITH (WHITAKER HOUSE)

UNION WITH GOD
BY JEANNE GUYON (CHRISTIAN BOOKS)

INTIMACY WITH THE BELOVED
BY PAT CHEN (CHARISMA HOUSE)

Renew Your Mind

Do not conform any longer to the pattern of this world, but be transformed by the renewing of your mind. Then you will be able to test and approve what God's will is – his good, pleasing and perfect will.

Romans 12:2

KEEP YOUR EYES ON THE MOUNTAIN TOP
by Paula White

Procuring the promises of God requires perseverance. Are you willing to press through adversity to fulfill your destiny?

Your life is about more than merely existing. You are pregnant with promises from God, and He has an assignment for you! But are you willing to endure the process to procure the blessings that are inside of you?

Joseph is the perfect example of a man who was pregnant with promise and yet had to walk through the processes, trials and hurts of life to attain his destiny. He was the son of Jacob and Rachel *(SEE GEN. 30:22-24)*. Because Joseph "was the son of his old age," Jacob loved him more than he did his other children, and he gave him a coat of many colors *(GEN. 37:3, NKJV)*.

Normally this type of coat was given only to the principal heir since it was a mark of high rank. In Jacob's family, it should have been given to the oldest son, Reuben, who was in line to receive the birthright.

Instead Joseph, the eleventh of twelve sons, was lifted to a place of authority over his brothers at the tender age of 17. Perhaps on the day he donned the coat, he sensed the destiny on his life. Maybe he felt he was going somewhere.

But there were circumstances that would prevent Joseph from walking in destiny. The Bible says that when Joseph's brothers saw the coat on him, they hated him and began to plot evil against him *(SEE V. 4)*.

As a Christian, you will find that when the enemy sees your blessings from God—when he gets a glimpse of your destiny—he wants to kill it. He wants to destroy the assignment God has given you, and he will bring people into your life whose only purpose is to hate you and attempt to defeat you.

He will also set up circumstances that are meant to distract and ultimately break you. He will send crises into your life at 5 years old that will keep you messed up when you are 50.

☞ *From Stumbling Block to Stepping Stone*

Like Joseph, I know firsthand what it is like to be rejected, betrayed, abandoned, cast aside and unloved.

Until I was 5 years old, I was Daddy's little girl—and a very happy child. But after my parents separated, my father committed suicide, and for many years afterward, I searched to find love again like the love I had received from him.

When I was 6 years old, I was horribly violated. In the weeks, months, and years that followed, the abuse was repeated again and again. I ran and hid for hours after each occurrence. I took long baths in an attempt to wash away the dirtiness.

Even after I became born again I struggled with my past. I lived like a person who was always expecting something to go wrong.

During the years, I learned an important lesson: God can take a stumbling block and turn it into a stepping stone. Now, instead of pitying myself when people and circumstances come against me, I look at hate and adversity as educational tools. I know that if I can discern the thing that other people hate about me, I will have discovered the thing that makes me valuable.

Another lesson I learned is that adversity always comes when you pursue your destiny, and the amount of success you have will depend on the amount of adversity you face. In other words, you will be rewarded for that which you endure.

It is important to understand that the enemy strategically schemes for you to be wounded because once you are wounded, disappointment sets in. The prefix "dis-" means "to move away from" or "to deprive of."

Appointment is your destiny with God. Disappointment takes you away from it. Disappointment often leads to discouragement, and when it does, the enemy succeeds in moving you away from your courage as well. Discouragement eventually leads to death— the death of your vision, your dreams and your destiny.

If you learn to recognize these obstructions, you will develop an attitude toward others that says, "I love you, but you're not going to kill me!" This will allow you to hold on to your vision, no matter who or what hurts or upsets you.

⚡ *Prepare for Opposition*

And you may be surprised by the source of the attacks, just as Joseph was surprised to be betrayed by his brothers. He didn't expect adversity to come from his own flesh and blood!

You too must learn to overcome the people who are closest to you. If they rejoice with you, praise God. But if they don't, you must press on in spite of them. Don't let anyone deter you from your destiny.

When Joseph went in search of his brothers at Dothan, they saw him from far off and conspired to kill him. Reuben's intervention spared his life, and instead of being murdered he was cast into a pit and sold as a slave to the Ishmaelites *(SEE GEN. 37:17-27)*. Eventually, Joseph was taken down to Egypt, where Potiphar, the captain of Pharaoh's guard, bought him *(SEE VV. 28,36)*.

Joseph had good reason to develop a victim mentality: He was betrayed by his own brothers and sent away from a father and a mother who loved him dearly. He was thrown into a dark, filthy pit and eventually sold as a slave to foreigners.

However, the Bible tells us that the Lord was with Joseph, and he became a successful man in the house of his Egyptian master. Even Potiphar noticed that the Lord caused all Joseph did to prosper *(SEE GEN. 39:2-3)*.

So Potiphar made Joseph his overseer, putting him in charge of all he had *(SEE V. 4)*. No matter what the enemy throws at us, God can turn it into good and get glory from even the most dire circumstance or situation.

But as often happens when things are looking good, the enemy—in the form of Potiphar's wife—showed up on the scene. After unsuccessfully attempting to seduce Joseph, she accused him of rape—and once again Joseph was cast into prison *(SEE VV. 7-20)*.

Still the Lord was with Joseph, showing him steadfast love and giving him favor in the sight of the keeper of the prison. Soon Joseph was put in charge of all the other prisoners *(SEE VV. 21-22)*.

Camper or Climber? Here we need to stop and examine Joseph's personality type. What kind of person could endure so much and yet not break? What made Joseph different?

Imagine yourself in a camp at the base of a mountain along with hundreds of other mountain climbers. Everyone is starting out with the same goal: to climb the mountain. Each person in the camp is given the same opportunity, the same basic equipment and an equal chance to accomplish the goal. But time soon shows us that there are three types of people in the camp. They are:

The Can't Doers. These folks start at the base of the mountain with everyone else, but they never even attempt the climb. They give up before the journey begins. They never do anything with their lives and constantly make excuses about why they shouldn't try to accomplish anything.

If their Daddy was poor, they figure they will be poor. If Mama had diabetes, they figure they'll have diabetes. They don't trust God enough to believe that they can do all things through Christ who strengthens them—so they stay at the base of the mountain, too fearful to step out.

The Campers. These folks begin climbing the mountain but as soon as adversity comes their way or things don't go quite the way they planned, they sit down and settle for second best. Yes, they attempt the climb, but they don't have the faith to hang in, press through and taste the goodness of God.

These are the people who will go out of their way to hold you back. They yell constantly at the folks up ahead explaining why it can't be done. And although they've had a taste of the goodness and an idea of what they are missing, they are too fearful to continue the climb.

The Climbers. These folks start out at the base of the hill with everyone else, but they are determined to make it to the top. They find strength in adversity and desire to taste fully the goodness of God.

If the wind blows cold and hard, they button up and keep on moving. If rocks fall about them, they duck their heads and keep on climbing. They keep pressing, they keep pursuing and they keep praising.

They seek the presence of God, and they are determined to be all He said they would be and to have all He promised they would have. They refuse to hear negative reports and choose to keep their eyes on Jesus. If you're part of this group, expect to catch hell—you'll have to face not only Satan and every devil who comes against you but also the Can't-Doers and the Campers.

Joseph was a climber. No matter what the enemy threw at him, he caught it and turned it into a touchdown. Even when he was in prison, he managed to turn lemons into lemonade.

One night the butler and the baker, who had been imprisoned by Pharaoh, each had dreams. Joseph interpreted their dreams and asked to be remembered when good fortune hit. Though the baker was hanged, the chief butler was restored, just as Joseph had predicted (SEE GEN. 40:5-22).

For a while, the butler forgot about Joseph (SEE V. 23). But when Pharaoh had a dream, the butler remembered the help he had received from Joseph and told Pharaoh about it (SEE GEN. 41:9-13). Joseph was summoned to Pharaoh's court, and Pharaoh was so pleased with his interpretations of the dream that he put his own signet ring upon Joseph's hand, arrayed him in fine garments, put gold chains around his neck and made him ride in his second chariot (SEE VV. 14-43). Moreover, he gave Joseph the wife of the priest of On to marry (SEE V. 45).

In time, Joseph was given an opportunity to exact revenge on his brothers, who had been the source of much pain in his life. However, he chose instead to walk in integrity and honor before God, and to bless and do good before all men.

He recognized that his whole life had been in God's hands and that it was God who had sent him to Egypt and preserved his life to be a blessing to His people in a time of famine. When his brothers came to him for food, he told them, "But, as for you, you meant evil against me; but God meant it for good, in order to bring it about as it is this day, to save many people alive" (GEN. 50:20).

So what kind of climber are you? Even if you have been a can't-doer or a camper in the past, it is possible to become a climber. You just have to move from sitting at the base of the mountain and begin heading toward the top. But how?

Discover your destiny. Do you know God's purpose for your life? Learn to unleash the power of the Holy Spirit and unlock the chains that hinder you from receiving the gifts God has for you.

Understand that the enemy will try to abort your dreams. He comes to steal, kill and destroy, but he has no power in your life. Your worship, praise, prayer and obedience can block the enemy from controlling your destiny.

Acknowledge that there is a process you must go through. You cannot get from the bottom of the mountain to the top without the climb. The process—the trials and the tests—qualify you for the promise.

Know that you can endure. Your strength comes from Him who is within you. Ask Him for what you need, and He will give it to you. And don't give up! If you set your sights on the mountaintop, He will make certain you get there. 🏵

 Paula White is the co-founder with her husband, Randy, of Without Walls International Church in Tampa, Florida. She ministers in churches and conferences and is the author of He Loves Me, He Loves Me Not *(Charisma House).*

For further study on this topic:

God Meant It for Good
by R. T. Kendall (Morning Star Publications)

Joseph: A Man of Absolute Integrity
by Charles Swindoll (Word)

A Woman's Guide to Getting Through Tough Times
by Quin Sherrer and Ruthanne Garlock (Vine Books)

LET US BOW BEFORE HIM
by Beth Moore

If we are to see the church strengthened and the nation healed, we must learn how to approach the throne of God in humble, reverent worship.

America is in a time of crisis. During the last several decades, more and more people have turned away from God, no longer wanting to hear what He has to say about their lives and circumstances. The result has been a frightening moral decline that threatens to destroy our country from the inside out.

Since the September 11 terrorist attacks, however, many ears have begun to open again. Fearful and uncertain about the future, many people are more willing than ever to listen to what God, through His church, has to say about the evil that has befallen our nation.

What a profound opportunity we have to see this nation turn back to God and to bring in a great harvest of souls! If we will cooperate with Him, God will turn the present evil to good and use it for His glory.

The key will be not how the depraved world responds to the crisis but how the church of Jesus Christ responds. What will we do with the opportunity God has placed before us?

Speaking for God Many people today are searching for God. They want to hear the voice of God, and they are looking to us to tell them what God is saying.

How do we dare speak for the God of all creation? How do we speak for the One who said, "Let there be..." and there was? The One whose voice is so strong, He literally sustains this world by the power of His word?

The thought of speaking for God should scare us to death—death to ourselves, death to our own agendas, and death to our own ideas and concepts and religion. God forbid that flesh should enter in when it's time to speak the words of God! Yet so often we say things without much prayer or thought, supposedly speaking for Him.

The Bible tells us, "Guard your steps when you go to the house of God. Go near to listen, rather than to offer the sacrifice of fools, who do not know that they do wrong. Do not be quick with your mouth, do not be hasty in your heart to utter anything before God. God is in heaven and you are on earth, so let your words be few.

"As a dream comes when there are many cares, so the speech of a fool when there are many words....Therefore stand in awe of God" (ECCL. 5:1-7, NIV).

By nightfall on September 11, religious commentators from all over the world were already speaking for God. Some of the words that were spoken may have been on target; others may not have been.

Certainly, in the immediate aftermath of the tragedy, there was a need for Christians to provide comfort in the midst of overwhelming devastation. But many were quick instead to utter the "opinions" of God. Was it time to speak His words? Where was the time spent standing in awe before Him first?

❧ Getting it Right

The world is listening to us right now as never before. That's why we must be careful to watch what we say.

Remember, Job's friends were quick to speak in his anguish; they had many noble things to say about his situation. Yet God ended that chapter of Job's life by declaring that the words those friends had spoken weren't right. As good and religious as their speeches sounded, they weren't the words of God.

Can preachers and teachers who have been right about God's words in the past suddenly be wrong when an urgent matter arises? I believe they can.

When King David told the prophet Nathan that he wanted to build a temple for God, Nathan thought the idea sounded good. Surely a house built in God's name would honor the Lord! And up to that point, Nathan had always been right; he had always accurately spoken the oracles of God. So he told David, "'Whatever you have in mind, go ahead and do it, for the Lord is with you'" (2 SAM. 7:3).

That night, however, God came to Nathan and told him that David was not supposed to build the temple; David's son, Solomon, would be the builder in the next generation. Nathan had to go back to David and retract the words he had spoken too quickly.

Just because any of us has been right in the past doesn't mean we are right now. Before we jump to a conclusion about what God would say in a given situation, we must first stand in awe of Him. We must let our words be few.

After all, God is in the heavens; we are here on Earth. We don't always know or understand how God is going to accomplish His perfect will. What makes sense and seems right to us now may not be right at all.

When Jesus was being taken away to be tried and crucified— and ultimately raised from the dead, completing the good work that was given to Him by the Father—Peter reacted by doing what he thought was right. In the urgency of the moment, he drew his sword and cut off a soldier's ear. But Jesus rebuked him for it.

You and I need to be careful not to do what Peter did. Yes, now is the time for believers to draw their swords of the Spirit and rise to face the challenge before us. But the question is, how will we use those swords?

Will we use them to cut off the ears of our hearers? Will we use them with meanness, speaking condemnation to such a degree that those who are dying to hear have their ears cut off instead?

To avoid such a mistake, we must not draw our swords until we have first stood in awe and listened for what it is that God wants to say in this hour. That should be our first response in any urgent matter: to stand in awe, be silent and listen.

⯌ *A Holy Fear*

We need to return to a holy fear of the Lord and a reverence for His Word! Remember how the people of Israel responded when Ezra read out loud the books of the Law? Nehemiah 8 tells us that as he opened the Scriptures, all the people stood up. Ezra praised the Lord, and all the people lifted their hands, cried "Amen!" and bowed down and worshiped.

I believe God is calling His church to fall on her face before Him again—not once, not just in this immediate crisis, but until the kingdom comes. It's time for us to put our faces to the ground in our congregations, in our homes and in our prayer closets. I'm not talking about a physical posture only; I'm talking about an attitude of the heart that demonstrates both humility and awe.

Many leaders have quoted 2 Chronicles 7:14 in recent months: "'If My people, who are called by My name, will humble themselves and pray and seek My face and turn from their wicked ways, then will I hear from heaven and will forgive their sin and will heal their land.'" What this Scripture tells us is that if we experience a lack of healing in our nation, it's not because unredeemed people are sinning. It's because Christians aren't bowing.

Healing and revival can come only as we, the church, bow down before Jesus and confess Him as Lord. We must do this long before we see Him face to face.

The truth is, if we say all the right things but have the wrong heart, God will not do battle for us. First Peter 5:5 says, "'God opposes the proud but gives grace to the humble.'" If we take our swords and speak the truth with pride and arrogance, God will oppose us, and our words will have no effect. If He sees our humility, however, He will raise up His mighty arm on our behalf. His grace and sufficiency will be with us and with the words we speak.

✺ God Rocked the House

Acts 4 tells the story of Peter and John being opposed by the religious rulers of the day strictly because they were servants of Jesus. The rulers initially released the two apostles after warning them "not to speak or teach at all in the name of Jesus" (ACTS 4:18).

Peter and John went back to the church and reported everything that the chief priests and elders had told them. When the believers heard the news, they did not draw their swords; instead, they raised their voices together in powerful prayer:

"'Sovereign Lord...You made the heaven and the earth and the sea, and everything in them. You spoke by the Holy Spirit through the mouth of Your servant, our father David: "Why do the nations rage and the people plot in vain? The kings of the earth take their stand and the rulers gather together against the Lord and against His Anointed One."

"'Indeed, Herod and Pontius Pilate met together with the Gentiles and the people of Israel in this city to conspire against Your holy servant Jesus, whom You anointed. They did what Your power and will had decided beforehand should happen. Now, Lord, consider their threats and enable Your servants to speak Your word with great boldness. Stretch out Your hand to heal and perform miraculous signs and wonders through the name of Your holy servant Jesus'" (Acts 4:24-30).

After they prayed, the Bible says, "the place where they were meeting was shaken. And they were all filled with the Holy Spirit and spoke the word of God boldly" (v. 31).

Do you want God to rock your house, your church, your nation, the way He rocked that first-century meeting place? Do you want Him to fill you with the Holy Spirit so you can speak His word with boldness? I know I do! The key is this: Before we speak—before we draw our swords—we must take time to stand in awe.

And it's important that we do that together. Acts 4:24 says the believers "raised their voices together in prayer to God." The Greek word translated together is actually a compound word meaning "same" and "mind" or "passion." From the beginning the church was birthed from among a very diverse people, and we are still diverse today.

We are never going to agree on all things. We have different gifts. But we have the same Lord.

If we are willing to come together with one mind and one passion—the passion to see God glorified and salvation multiplied —then God will rock the house. If we come together as a church in this nation across all denominational, ethnic and racial barriers; if we choose to humble ourselves before God and be unified in His name; if we cry out together with like passion; then He will be glorified, and salvation will be multiplied. His Spirit will fill us, and each one of us will boldly speak His word.

❧ *A Great Outpouring*

Acts 2:17-18 tells us that the greatest outpouring of the Holy Spirit of all time will be characterized by the bold proclamation of God's Word. Neighbor to neighbor, friend to friend, parent to child, believers will not hesitate to tell others about Jesus. They will live with the Word of God fresh upon their tongues and burning in their hearts.

In that day, they will stand in awe. They will listen. They will bow down. Only then will they draw the sword.

Our nation is in crisis, and people are open to hearing what God has to say to them in the midst of their confusion and fear. We need an outpouring of the Holy Spirit so that you and I can speak the word of God to them—the word that is right for this critical hour; the word that will cut to their hearts, not cut off their ears.

As Christians, we have a lot to say that the world needs to hear. People need to know that God is sovereign and Jesus is Lord—now more than ever.

But let's determine not to speak too quickly. Before we draw the sword, let us first stand in awe. ❀

Beth Moore is a writer and teacher of best-selling Bible studies whose public speaking engagements carry her all over the world. A dedicated wife and mother of two, Moore lives in Houston with her husband, Keith. Her most recent release is When Godly People Do Ungodly Things *(Broadman & Holman).*

FOR FURTHER STUDY ON THIS TOPIC:

JESUS THE ONE AND ONLY
BY BETH MOORE (LIFEWAY PRESS)

PLACED IN HIS GLORY
BY FUCHSIA PICKETT (CHARISMA HOUSE)

VISION OF HIS GLORY
BY ANNE GRAHAM LOTZ (W PUBLISHING GROUP)

WHEN WE WANDER FROM GOD
by Iverna Tompkins

I chose a path that led away from God, but in His mercy He protected me and drew me back. He can do the same for you.

One muggy day in the Nevada desert, Espie and Beulah Cornwall and their two toddlers were driving from their home in Reno to the distant town where Espie, a small-church pastor, was scheduled to minister. The 3-year-old, Robert, had fallen asleep in Beulah's lap in the front seat; Judson, 5, sat alone in the back. All was peaceful and quiet until the sound of fervent prayer from the back seat broke the silence.

"What are you praying for?" Beulah asked.

"A baby sister," Judson responded.

Mrs. Cornwall was silent. In the Cornwall family five generations had failed to produce a girl, and she had little hope that she would be the one to break that trend. But in the following months, Judson continued to both pray and declare that he was going to have a sister.

When Beulah discovered she was expecting a child, she wondered if Judson's prayers would be answered. She dreaded the thought of disappointing him with another brother.

But on August 22, 1929, a baby girl was born to the Cornwalls. I was named Iverna, after my mother's sister. No one shouted louder than Judson, who did not hesitate to remind his parents, "I told you!"

❧ Protected for a Purpose

The Scriptures tell us that each of us is known by God; each of us is born with a purpose. "For You formed my inward parts; You covered me in my mother's womb...Your eyes saw my substance, being yet unformed. And in Your book they all were written, the days fashioned for me, when as yet there were none of them" *(Ps. 139:13,16, NKJV)*. I know that as I look back over my own life—the life my brother Judson so fervently prayed into existence—I'm amazed at the way God not only gives us purpose, but also protects us, directs us and enables us to fulfill that purpose.

After I was born, my parents had two more children—both sons. There were benefits in being the only girl of the family, but there were disadvantages, too. At bedtime, the two older boys went to their room and the two younger ones to theirs; Mother and Dad had each other; but I had no one.

However, it was in my aloneness that I learned to have a personal relationship with Jesus. Talking with Him became so natural and intimate that it was years later before I realized this was unusual for someone so young.

The enemy realized it, though, and tried to incite me to fear. As soon as I was alone in my room, he would declare his presence and speak threats. Often a hairy hand would grab mine, a dark cloud would fill the room and panic would overwhelm me.

One night when I cried out because of the evil presence, my mother told some friends who were visiting about the problem and suggested that they pray together for deliverance. At the time I was lying still in my bed, afraid of being touched by the hairy hand. Suddenly a white cloud with a gold lining seemed to float into my room through the closed window and hover over my bed. Such peace filled me that all fear departed from that night forward.

It was sometime later, at the age of 8, that I felt the conviction of the Holy Spirit while listening to my dad preach. I ran to the altar and wept my way to a true born-again experience. Interestingly, it was not a time of renewal in the church.

Yet the Lord put such a hunger in me to be filled that I cried out at the altar long after most others had left the service. When His glory came it filled not only the little girl seeking but also the few others who remained, and true revival began.

As a young girl, ministry was just "living" to me, whether I was holding church services in the basement for my little friends or tossing apples to the prisoners in the jail and telling them about Jesus through the bars. A new vista opened up, however, when my mother and I went to visit my aunt and uncle, Ross and Iverna Lamb, who ministered among the Indians in northern California.

To my surprise, my uncle invited me to preach in their church on a Sunday night.

"What should I say?" I asked.

"Why, I don't know," he answered wisely. "You'd better ask Jesus."

I went to my room and prayed, and the Lord gave me a message that He used that night to minister to the people. I rejoiced as many accepted Jesus and were filled with the Holy Spirit.

Shortly after returning home, a pastor phoned saying that he had heard I was available for meetings. He wanted me to come to his church! Fearfully, I obeyed—and I have been traveling in ministry ever since.

☙ A Wayward Path

For several years my family traveled throughout Oregon planting churches; then we settled in Vallejo, California, where my dad pastored an Assembly of God church. One by one the three oldest children left home to attend Bible college, and both Judson and Robert married.

My life, however, did not fall into place as easily as my brothers'. I had some disappointing relationships, left school and became part of a church staff. There, I experienced deep discouragement and ended up walking out of the church declaring, "If that is how they treat Christians, I want no part of it." Hurt and frustrated, I allowed bitterness and hatred to fill my heart for the first time in my life.

I began dating unbelievers and ultimately fell in love with one and married him. Life seemed easy for a while, but I was aware that something was missing. Although I often found myself witnessing to people in need, I had no prayer life, didn't read the Word and was always glad to share my bitterness about Christians.

It was during my pregnancy that I faced the truth and acknowledged that I needed God's help. I returned to church but felt nothing. My husband was overseas with the armed services,

and although I attempted to regain my precious time with Jesus,
I felt empty and alone.

One day I asked Him, "Why do I feel nothing?"

"You walked away; you can walk back," I heard Him say.

A new determination gripped me, and day after day I prayed
and read my Bible. One day while driving to my job I heard myself
declare, "I may never cry again or feel Your presence, but I will
spend eternity with You because Your Word promises that!"

Tears flowed as though a dam had burst; joy replaced the
barrenness I'd known. That experience has been a deterrent against
backsliding through the years, and I have never ceased to be
grateful for His presence.

I wish I could say that my marriage improved when I turned
back to the Lord, but in fact it deteriorated. I lacked wisdom in
sharing the changes that were taking place in me, and my husband
and I found less and less interest in each other's lives. After 10
years of marriage, and following the births of my daughter and
son, he left one final time.

Only God knows the guilt and devastation I felt. There I was,
the only girl in my family—and a disgrace to our name because I
had dropped out of school, divorced my husband, and now faced
the prospect of raising two children alone with no financial support!

ஐ *Prepared for His Service*

Like many of us when we learn the lessons of life, I often
failed to see my experiences as preparation for God's call. Because
of the wrong path I had taken, I instead saw every problem I
encountered as something I deserved.

With each one, the Lord would remind me of His call on my
life, confirming it over and over using John 15:16: "You did not
choose Me, but I chose you and appointed you that you should
go and bear fruit." But I dismissed the word. Because of my failures, I was sure it was too late.

I didn't realize then that my taking classes at night, working
full-time in probation work and donating time as a youth and

music director in a small church while mothering were all part of God's training. I didn't know that I was going to move to Oregon to become an assistant to my brother Judson. I didn't know that as I helped him I was tiptoeing toward the fulfillment of God's purpose for me.

I was comfortable being in the shelter of my big brother in ministry—and then God began to take him away. Judson's ministry grew to be in great demand throughout the world. He spent less and less time in the local church until I ended up with the entire responsibility of pastoring. Proverbs 18:16 says, "A man's gift makes room for him," and I was living proof of that.

Although I was a woman and a divorcee, the anointing of the Holy Spirit broke every fetter of prejudice and discrimination and made a place for me. Times of discouragement came, but God remained faithful.

When David Schoch called me out in a meeting and prophesied that the Lord was sending me out to the whole body of Christ, he admonished me never to ask for a meeting by letter or phone. He also said that I must not look back because everything that had preceded this moment was but a school.

I had no idea how the Lord was going to accomplish all that was spoken in the prophecy, but I knew that He was going to fulfill His Word—and He has. During the last 25 years, I have ministered in 11 nations and most of the United States. I have written 11 books and made thousands of tapes. In 1989, Sweetwater Bible College conferred on me an honorary doctoral degree.

When God makes a way, it's a big way!

I encourage you to look back over your life and recognize the hand of God leading you into the awesome purpose He has uniquely planned for you. Rest assured; God is faithful.

Nothing you have done—no mistakes you have made—can disqualify you. As Paul said, "He who has begun a good work in you will complete it until the day of Jesus Christ" *(PHIL. 1:6).* You were born with a purpose! 🏵

Iverna Tompkins is founder and president of Iverna Tompkins Ministries, a leadership training ministry based in Scottsdale, Arizona. She ministers regularly with Women of the Word conferences and is the author of several books, including All in God's Time *(Charisma House).*

PHOEBE PALMER
by Joseph W. Martin

Phoebe Palmer was born in New York City on December 18, 1807, and raised in a strict Methodist family. During her early years, she struggled in her religious life because she could not define a specific conversion experience in the traditional Methodist sense.

In 1827, Phoebe married Walter Clarke Palmer, a highly respected physician. During the first 10 years of their marriage, the Palmers suffered a great deal. They lost three of their first four children.

Phoebe's religious search for the deep emotional experience she had observed in others intensified, as did her guilt and grief over the death of her first two sons. She saw their deaths as a judgment from God for her lack of full devotion.

In 1831, the Palmers opened up their home to Phoebe's sister Sarah and her husband. Sarah exercised a positive influence on Phoebe, involving her in religious studies, prayer meetings and gatherings.

In 1835, these meetings resulted in the establishment of a Bible study held every Tuesday at the Palmers' home. These meetings became known as the "Tuesday meetings for the promotion of holiness."

During this time Phoebe lost her second daughter, Eliza, due to a fire in the nursery. Although the experience was tragic, God comforted Phoebe. Soon her grief was replaced by a song of praise.

Two years after the death of Eliza, Phoebe finally declared herself "entirely devoted to God." From this point on, her life was endued with an increase of spiritual power.

In 1840, Phoebe took over the leadership of the Tuesday meetings. They laid the groundwork for her teachings on holiness, consecration, and "entire sanctification" or "second blessing," which Pentecostals later called "the baptism of the Holy Spirit."

During the years when Phoebe's ministry grew, many Methodist bishops and leaders attended her meetings. She began to draw great national and international interest.

Phoebe traveled with her husband throughout the United States, Canada and England, teaching and preaching. Her meetings were marked with great power, and thousands of people experienced remarkable conversions.

Known also for writing, Phoebe authored poetry and hymns and published best-selling books. She also edited a magazine, *The Guide to Holiness,* until her death in 1874.

Phoebe Palmer's teaching ministry helped lay the foundation of the Holiness movement. Later, the Pentecostal/charismatic movement sprang up, utilizing much of the terminology and theology that Phoebe had espoused earlier. In a real sense, Phoebe Palmer can be considered the spiritual mother of both movements. ❀

Joseph Martin is a Pentecostal historian-researcher and is the Resource Director at Victory Bible Institute in Tulsa, Oklahoma. He has compiled The Spirit-Filled Woman *devotional (Charisma House) along with several other books.*

GRIEVE NOT THE SPIRIT
by Phoebe Palmer

God desires for us to be sensitive to the things that are contrary to His nature.

Daily my heart is cleaving more closely to Christ and getting more detached from earthly objects. The weaning process is going on. I find the closer I get to the heart of Infinite Love—the nearer to the Sun of Righteousness—the more sensitively do I feel, to my heart's deepest core, everything that is contrary in spirit, word or action to the law of love.

If we do, indeed, get nearer to the Sun of Righteousness, we cannot help but see with greater vividness everything that is unrighteous and unlovely. And then the sight of the eyes will affect the heart.

What must the sufferings of the Savior have been during His sojourn on earth! How continuously must His gentle, pure spirit have been lacerated! I have seldom had such a perception of what the keenness of His sufferings must have been, as since I have been pursuing the above train of thought. It appears as though His entire stay on earth, from childhood to His expiring groan on the cross, must have been one continuous crucifixion.

So it is for us when we are one with Him. But others do not always perceive or understand our heightened sensitivity.

"Do you feel such things?" someone once asked me, after having been the means of subjecting me to a humiliation which, had it not been for its religious association, would have branded him as exceedingly uncourteous. From his manner in proposing this inquiry, I presume he thought my professions of deadness to the world involved a deadness of all the finer sensibilities of the soul.

His misperception may have been based on his observation of the way those who are truly sanctified in body, soul and spirit endure woundings of the spirit—with a lamb-like, uncomplaining temper.

They receive with only slight outward manifestations of pain things that before would have been avenged or in some way resented. In imitation of their divine Redeemer, they, "as a sheep dumb before her shearers," open not their mouths.

But if this silent submission has been regarded as an intimation that the uncomplaining one does not feel or has not been wounded —how greatly the reverse is the fact!

He has been wounded, and far more deeply wounded than your oft-blunted sensibilities can imagine. He retires noiselessly because He whom he serves has said, "The servant of the Lord must not strive."

𝔰 *God Will Avenge*

You may never again on earth hear about your unloving words and actions, but are they untold? It is true they may never be breathed in mortal ear, but shall they remain unrevealed? No! "Their angels do always behold the face of My Father" *(MATT. 18:10, KJV)*.

An unseen messenger was standing by, and, as you gave the causeless offense, that winged messenger went with speed and told it directly to the ear of God. And will the triune God hear it, and take cognizance of the act? Yes! And He will avenge. True as God is true, retribution awaits you.

"Vengeance is mine," saith the Lord *(ROM. 12:19)*. "Whoso shall offend one of these little ones which believe in Me, it were better for him that a millstone were hanged about his neck, and that he were drowned in the depth of the sea" *(MATT. 18:6)*.

It is a meek and quiet spirit with whom you have contended, and since God gave that spirit it is of great price in His sight. It ought to have been of great price in your sight as well.

Do you persecute Christ? Christ's persecutors are not always those who are of the world.

Perhaps you are an erring child of God. Your wife, your husband, your child, your brother or sister, or perchance some friend with whom you have been closely affiliated has entered into the enjoyment of perfect love. You have witnessed his increasing deadness to the world. Things that, at one time, he could enjoy in common with yourself, now pain his heart, while from the depths of his soul, he cries out to God, "Turn away mine eyes from beholding vanity" *(Ps. 119:37)*.

Following Christ, the Light of Life, his soul is becoming more and more conformed to His image. He loves the things God loves and hates the things He hates.

How uneasy these marked preferences have made you! Because you cannot get him to see as you see and do as you do, with how many unkind allusions have you pained the loving heart of that gentle one, whom, in defiance of yourself, you cannot help but love and admire!

Conscience tells you that you are wrong, and you know it. Still you persist. Your opposition, perhaps, may be merely fitful— yet you continue to oppose, and as the occasion arises, you infer, by your unloving allusions and by silent action and innuendo, that you intend to offend that gentle, loving heart, whose every pulsation is in unison with God for your good.

O, do so no more, not only because "their angels do always behold the face of their Father," but because you are sinning against your own soul's best interest! God is love. Every unloving look, word or action is an abhorrence to Him.

"By the love of the Spirit," I beseech you, "grieve not the Spirit" *(SEE EPH. 4:30)*. Would a dear friend, however intent on your good, abide with you, if the feelings of his sensitive heart were continually being attacked by oft-repeated assaults? So the Spirit will not always strive.

Recognize that you are in danger. Seven other spirits worse than the first may enter. And what will you do, should that fearful hour come upon you without the aid of the Spirit whom you have grieved away? Let him that standeth take heed lest he fall.

Be assured, by one who knows, that the restiveness you feel when the stricter forms of piety are presented before you is most evidently indicative of the remains of the carnal mind. "The flesh lusteth against the Spirit" *(GAL. 5:17)*.

If you yield to it, you sin against God. For in sinning against His people, you sin against Christ as though He were here in person. By the light of a truly Christian example, you have been reproved. Acknowledge your error, and seek a holy heart. 🌸

 Phoebe Palmer (1807-1874) was a forerunner of both the Holiness and the Pentecostal/charismatic movements. This selection is adapted from Incidental Illustrations of the Economy of Salvation *by Phoebe Palmer. Published by Henry V. Degen, Boston, 1855.*

WHEN YOU PRAY, BELIEVE

by Andrew Murray

It's one thing to pray; it's another to be assured you have what you ask for. What is the secret of believing prayer?

When Jesus was on Earth, He made an incredible promise to His disciples regarding prayer that is recorded in Mark 11:24: "'Therefore I say to you, whatever things you ask when you pray, believe that you receive them, and you will have them'" *(NKJV)*. This promise of answer to prayer is one of the most wonderful in all Scripture. But in how many hearts has it raised the question: However can I attain the faith that knows it receives all it asks?

It is this question our Lord would answer today. Before He gave that wonderful promise to His disciples, He spoke another word, in which He points out where the faith in the answer to prayer originates and ever finds its strength. "'Have faith in God. For assuredly, I say to you, whoever...does not doubt in his heart, but believes that those things he says will be done, he will have whatever he says'" *(v. 23)*.

"Have faith in God." This word precedes the other, "Have faith in the promise of an answer to prayer."

The power to believe a promise depends entirely on faith in the promiser. Trust in the person begets trust in his word.

It is only where we live and associate with God in personal, loving intercourse, where God Himself is all to us, where our whole being is continually opened up and exposed to the mighty influences that are at work, where His holy presence is revealed, that the capacity will be developed for believing that He gives whatsoever we ask.

This connection between faith in God and faith in His promise will become clear to us if we think what faith really is. It is often compared to the hand or the mouth, by which we take and appropriate what is offered to us.

But it is important to understand that faith is also the ear by which I hear what is promised, the eye by which I see what is offered me. On this the power to take depends.

I must hear the person who gives me the promise: The very tone of his voice gives me courage to believe. I must see him: In the light of his eye and countenance all fear as to my right to take passes away. The value of the promise depends on the promiser: It is on my knowledge of what the promiser is that faith in the promise depends.

It is for this reason that Jesus, before He gives that wonderful prayer-promise, first says, "Have faith in God." That is, let your eye be open to the living God, and gaze on Him, seeing Him who is invisible.

Believing God is just looking to God and what He is, allowing Him to reveal His presence, giving Him time and yielding the whole being to take in the full impression of what He is as God.

Faith is the eye to which God shows what He is and does. Through faith the light of His presence and the workings of His mighty power stream into the soul. As that which I see lives in me, so by faith God lives in me too.

And even so faith is also the ear through which the voice of God is always heard and intercourse with Him kept up. It is through the Holy Spirit the Father speaks to us. The Son is the Word, the substance of what God says; the Spirit is the living voice.

This the child of God needs to lead and guide him. The secret voice from heaven must teach him, as it taught Jesus, what to say and what to do. An ear opened toward God—a believing heart waiting on Him, to hear what He says—will hear Him speak.

The words of God will be more than the words of a Book; proceeding from the mouth of God, they will be spirit and truth, life and power. They will bring in deed and living experience what are otherwise only thoughts.

When faith now is in full exercise as eye and ear, as the faculty of the soul by which we see and hear God, then it will be able to exercise its full power as hand and mouth, by which we appropriate God and His blessings. The power of reception will depend entirely on the power of spiritual perception. For this reason Jesus said, before He gave the promise that God would answer believing prayer: "Have faith in God."

Faith is simply surrender: I yield myself to the impression the tidings I hear make on me. By faith I yield myself to the living God. His glory and love fill my heart and have the mastery over my life.

Faith is fellowship; I give myself up to the influence of the friend who makes me a promise and become linked to him by it. And it is when we enter into this living fellowship with God Himself, in a faith that always sees and hears Him, that it becomes easy and natural to believe His promise as to prayer.

Faith in the promise is the fruit of faith in the promiser: The prayer of faith is rooted in the life of faith. And in this way the faith that prays effectually is indeed a gift of God—not as something that He bestows or infuses at once, but in a far deeper and truer sense, as the blessed disposition or habit of soul which is wrought and grows up in us in a life of intercourse with Him. Surely for one who knows his Father well, and lives in constant close intercourse with Him, it is a simple thing to believe the promise that He will do the will of His child who lives in union with Himself.

It is because very many of God's children do not understand this connection between the life of faith and the prayer of faith that their experience of the power of prayer is so limited. When they desire earnestly to obtain an answer from God, they fix their whole heart upon the promise and try their utmost to grasp that promise in faith. When they do not succeed, they are ready to give up hope; the promise is true but is beyond their power to take hold of it in faith.

Listen to the lesson Jesus teaches us this day: Have faith in God, the living God. Let faith look to God more than to the thing promised; it is His love, His power, His living presence that will awaken the faith.

A physician would say, to one asking for some means to get more strength in his arms and hands to seize and hold, that his whole constitution must be built up and strengthened. In the same way, the cure for a feeble faith is to be found in the invigoration of our whole spiritual life by intercourse with God. Learn to believe in God, to take hold of God, to let God take possession of your life, and it will be easy to take hold of the promise. He who knows and trusts God finds it easy to trust the promise too.

God's promise will be to us what God Himself is. It is the man who walks before the Lord and falls on his face to listen while the living God speaks to him who will really receive the promise.

Though we have God's promises in the Bible, with full liberty to take them, the spiritual power is wanting, except as God Himself speaks them to us. And He speaks to those who walk and live with Him.

Therefore, have faith in God. Let faith be all eye and ear, the surrender to let God make His full impression and reveal Himself fully in the soul.

Count it one of the chief blessings of prayer to exercise faith in God as the living, mighty God who waits to fulfill in us all the good pleasure of His will and the work of faith with power. See in Him the God of Love, whose delight it is to bless and impart Himself.

In such worship of faith in God the power will speedily come to believe the promise too: "Whatever things you ask when you pray, believe that you receive them." When you do in faith make God your own, the promise will be yours too.

The precious lesson that Jesus has to teach us this day is this: We seek God's gifts; but God wants to give us Himself first. We think of prayer as the power to draw down good gifts from heaven, Jesus as the means to draw ourselves up to God. We want to stand at the door and cry; Jesus would have us first enter in and realize that we are friends and children.

Let us accept the teaching. Let every experience of the littleness of our faith in prayer urge us first to have and exercise more faith in the living God, and in such faith to yield ourselves to Him. A heart full of God has power for the prayer of faith. Faith in God begets faith in the promise, in the promise too of an answer to prayer.

Therefore, child of God, take time, take time, to bow before Him, to wait on Him to reveal Himself. Take time, and let your soul in holy awe and worship exercise and express its faith in the Infinite One, and as He imparts Himself and takes possession of you, the prayer of faith will crown your faith in God. ✤

 Andrew Murray (1828-1917) was an ordained minister in the Dutch Reformed Church of South Africa and the author of numerous devotional works that have become classics, including Abide in Christ, Absolute Surrender *and* With Christ in the School of Prayer.

FOR FURTHER STUDY ON THIS TOPIC:

DRAWING CLOSER TO GOD'S HEART
BY EDDIE AND ALICE SMITH (CHARISMA HOUSE)

PRAYING GOD'S WORD
BY BETH MOORE (BROADMAN & HOLMAN)

REES HOWELLS INTERCESSOR
BY NORMAN GRUBB (CHRISTIAN LITERATURE CRUSADE)

SEASONS OF A WOMAN'S LIFE
by *Thetus Tenney*

*You don't have to do all things at all times.
God has ordained seasons of fruitfulness
for you.*

She was the wife of a young pastor with a thriving congregation. Heavily involved in the church, she had been a vital key to its spiritual vibrancy and growth. She was also the soon-to-be mother of her second child.

"Before I heard your message, I felt frustrated and guilty," she admitted to me. "On the one hand, I saw the ministry needs of the people around me. On the other, I knew I had a new baby on the way who would need my attention and nurture.

"But after listening to your teaching," she said, "I felt every part of my body and spirit begin to relax. It was suddenly clear to me that this period of life is only for a season."

That had been my topic: seasons. They were, after all, God's idea: "While the earth remains, seedtime and harvest, cold and heat, winter and summer, and day and night shall not cease" (GEN. 8:22, NKJV).

The fact is no woman is called to do all things at all times. Seasons are an integral part of God's program for the earth— and for people.

This was recognized by the psalmists, the prophets and the apostles. Fruit comes in due season, and so do tears (PS. 1:3; 22:2). Rainy days come in seasons (JER. 5:24; EZEK. 34:26). Prophetic words are fulfilled in their season (LUKE 1:20). There are seasons of heaviness and seasons of rejoicing (1 PET. 1:6).

It seems that God in His wisdom punctuated all of life with seasons. And just as punctuation marks add meaning and variety to written communication, causing the reader to pause for understanding, accelerate with excitement or end abruptly at the conclusion, so seasons bring necessary meaning and variety to our lives.

After all, can you imagine what life would be like if it were merely one long day? One sameness?

The wise man of Ecclesiastes declares, "To everything there is a season" *(Eccl. 3:1)*. In nature there is a progression from winter to spring to summer to fall. In our lives, too, there is a progression of change from one season to another. As surely as seasons direct the course of nature, so they direct the courses of our lives.

Understanding and accepting this can bring contentment. As Paul said, "For I have learned in whatever state I am, to be content" *(Phil. 4:11)*. If we cooperate with the seasons of life, we can experience great productivity and fruitfulness. But if we struggle against them, we will be constantly anxious and frustrated.

Physically, seasons are inevitable. Time, measured in years, directs our changing course from infancy to the edge of immortality. Slowly nature etches the lines of maturity on the countenance of inexperience.

Tiring trivia, so necessary in the young years of building homes, families, careers and ministries, gives way to quiet knowing. Wisdom and patience compensate for waning strength and failing energy. Graceful reconciliation with the changing years brings serenity and an experienced trust.

Every season, from youth to old age, has its own responsibilities and rewards. Primary responsibilities change in various seasons, and as they do, new opportunities become available. If we are sensitive to the varying responsibilities of each season, we can reap the reward of a greater harvest in seasons to come.

✿ Ranking Priorities

For women of vision and accountability, the child-rearing years often produce undue pressure. Possessing ability and giftedness—and stimulated by a vast array of "you-can-do-it" books and "you-should-be-doing-it" seminars—many young mothers become frustrated. Understanding the principle of seasons, however, can alleviate the guilt, help chart a course for the future and give children the direction they need, too.

If you have children at home, realize this: It is for only a short season! Responsibilities attended to well during the early years of motherhood can produce an extended harvest for the kingdom through the lives of your children. On the other hand, neglect during this season can produce wild tares and weeds for you to contend with in the seasons to come.

With clear perspective, determine how much extended involvement you can manage, and do not feel guilty or repressed by your decision. Feel comfortable with the ranking order of your priorities, knowing that this season will pass and your present priorities will change.

I first met Joy Strang, the publisher of *SpiritLed Woman*, at a women's leadership conference several years ago. Anyone who knew Joy recognized immediately she was not out of place at a leadership meeting. However, a few years lapsed before she became as visibly involved in leading women as she is today.

Why? One reason: Seasons. Joy was the mother of a 1-year-old boy at the time of that conference.

My life, too, has been punctuated by seasons. As a young mother I experienced the season of long hours at home with my children. My husband, Tom, was in a traveling ministry, and since our house was in a wooded area with few neighbors, I had little involvement with others and felt quite tied down.

My natural motivation urged me to be up, out and away. But my primary responsibilities in those early years of marriage and family determined the season of my life. Feeling alone and stifled, I sometimes battled with resentment and frustration.

The conflict was resolved, however, when I determined to fill some of the lonely hours with reading and study that would benefit me for the future. A studious mind helped a lonely heart!

Before going to bed each night, I would set the house in order for the next day. Then I'd get up very early the next morning and have several hours of undisturbed prayer and study before my motherly duties demanded my attention.

I read many books. I even read Bible commentaries! This was a season which, in retrospect, passed much more quickly than it seemed at the time.

I have now lived full circle. Today I have few home and family responsibilities. I am free to work, travel and speak. Little did I realize, while taking care of my primary responsibility as a young mother, that I had also been given an opportunity that would develop my future ministry of teaching and writing!

Those years of study became the foundation for my life's work. Never have I had another season for such intense reading, study and prayer without the simultaneous pressure of producing. Those were tough years—but good ones.

My advice to all young mothers with a heart for ministry is this: Do what you can now. Plan and prepare for the future, but do not feel guilty and overload yourself during the formative years of your marriage and children. It is an important season with important priorities. Tend it well. Another season will come—and you will be prepared.

☞ *Grand Central Station*

For me, a new season dawned when my children became teen-agers. Before then, I had always enjoyed cooking and entertaining fellow ministers and workers in my home. Those times of hospitality and fellowship were special for the entire family.

However, the teen years turned our home into Grand Central Station for the high school crowd. My plans and my teen-agers' plans frequently conflicted.

During this season Tom and I decided it was more important for our home to be open and ready for the younger set than for us to entertain our peers with lovely dinners. Tacos, hamburgers, the Colonel's chicken, lots of cookies and gallons of milk became our home entertainment fare, replacing beautiful roasted meats with Yorkshire pudding, ham and asparagus rolls, and minted tea.

It was a season of making memories we still share with a large circle of now-grown-up young friends. I have never regretted one evening that I gave up studying or speaking in order to sit on the floor in our basement den with my husband, our children and their friends, discussing in lively fashion whatever the issue of the moment was. It was a short season, never to be recaptured. I'm glad I didn't miss it!

☙ People in Progress

Just as there are seasons in nature, in the physical body and in our life's work, there are also spiritual seasons. They are a part of the production process of the kingdom.

Each one of us experiences times of plowing, sowing and harvesting, with all the attendant challenges and pleasures. The budding of a ministry with a fresh anointing is filled with expectancy. The blossoming time brings expectancy into recognition. The season of bearing fruit necessitates the work of preservation and sharing. Harvest is attended with great joy.

And according to the law of production, fruit-bearing is rewarded with the repetition of the process. Our fruit becomes more fruit and progresses to the bounteous harvest of much fruit.

It is important to remember, however, that a cycle of production is often preceded by a dormant season. This is a time during which it seems as if nothing is happening spiritually—when we feel stripped bare, buried in isolation, forgotten. Such a time came to the Apostle John on the island of Patmos and to the Apostle Paul in prison.

It may come to you in a time of sickness, loss, disappointment or rejection. I can assure you it will come—but only for a season. Be mindful that every bleak winter carries with it the promise of another spring.

Whatever season you find yourself in, practice patience, and know that He who began the work in you is able to complete it (SEE PHIL. 1:6). Patience is what keeps faith working. And refrain from judging yourself or others harshly in present circumstances.

We are not all at the same stage of development—nor are we all destined to produce the same crop. Some crops require a longer growing season. Besides, who would determine the worth of a fruit tree in the wintertime, while it is barren and leafless? We are all people-in-progress!

But while a force beyond yourself determines your season, your reaction to the season is your responsibility. God determines when a particular season comes; your responsibility is to tend what has been planted.

We would be foolish to try to plant in winter or harvest in spring. Yet we often resist the circumstances God has allowed to promote growth!

☞ Stormy Weather

In every season, of course, storms may appear. You may be dancing on a sunbeam when the ring of the telephone comes like a clap of thunder, bearing unexpected news of calamity or loss. Even the best seasons of life can be clouded by a storm.

At such times, thank God for the promise in His Word—that wonderful phrase of Scripture found 120 times within 120 verses, or 10 times for each month: "It shall come to pass." Storms come, and storms pass. They don't last forever. The sun will shine again!

The passing years and seasons, I've found, have galvanized my emotions. I know now that not every storm will sink my ship. (Hopefully, none of them will!) I also know that when the storm is raging, my feelings are not sure ground.

I take heart in God's comments to Job—the man of many seasons, serial storms and bounteous blessings. There are treasures in the snow, God told Job, and hail is reserved for the days of trouble, wars, and battle. I have learned that today's tempest often will hold the sustenance and strength for the future. Storms can make channels for the rain, and tender new growth comes as a result of the storm (SEE JOB 38:22-23,25-27).

Paul said we comfort others "with the comfort with which we ourselves are comforted by God" (2 COR. 1:4). The increasing fruitfulness of subsequent seasons, from which we nurture others, may often be augmented by the experience of a storm.

So whatever season of life you are in, make full use of it! Even a dormant season can become a special time for needed rest, quiet listening to God and fresh study. Don't waste time wishing you were someone else, somewhere else, doing something else.

This is a futile exercise. God made you as you are to use you as He planned. Living fully in your present is the best insurance for your future.

Understanding the law of seasons can relieve whatever pressure you feel about your current circumstances and increase your faith for the future. While we anticipate the fruit, we must understand the process: You will bring forth fruit in due season *(SEE PS. 1:13)*. Don't despair; the day of reaping will come! ❀

 Thetus Tenney is a women's ministry director, speaker and author of several books on prayer. She has held numerous leadership roles within the United Pentecostal Church. A booklet on the subject of this article is available from Focused Light Ministries, P.O. Box 55, Tioga, LA 71477.

FOR FURTHER STUDY ON THIS TOPIC:

ALL IN GOD'S TIME
BY IVERNA TOMPKINS (CHARISMA HOUSE)

MOTHERS TOGETHER
BY RUTH BELL GRAHAM AND GIGI GRAHAM TCHIVIDJIAN (BAKER)

PERENNIAL
BY TWILA PARIS (ZONDERVAN)

CATHERINE BOOTH
by Joseph W. Martin

FORERUNNERS OF FAITH
Mother of the Salvation Army

On Jan. 17, 1829, Catherine Mumford was born at Ashbourne, Derbyshire, England. Her mother was a model of Methodist piety and raised Catherine to be very devout in her faith. Her father was a carriage maker and lay Methodist preacher who struggled with alcoholism.

Early in life, Catherine developed an intensely compassionate nature and began devoting herself to reading and studying the Bible. During her childhood she was very sick but managed to read through the entire Bible eight times before the age of 12.

At 14, though mostly bedridden, Catherine began writing articles about the abuses of alcoholism.

She was 22 when she met William Booth, who had come to preach at her church. They were married in 1855 and had eight children, most of whom would later hold positions in the Salvation Army.

Catherine was her husband's most loyal supporter and often accompanied him on his evangelistic travels. She began working with children and youth and meeting with women's societies.

As a result of the influence of Phoebe Palmer, an American minister, Catherine became convinced of a woman's right to preach the gospel. In 1859 she published the pamphlet, *Female Ministry*. But she didn't actually begin preaching until 1860 when, during a service at her husband's church, she rose and gave a sermon that was so impressive it changed William's mind about women preachers.

In 1864, the Booths established an outreach in London's East End called the Christian Mission, which later developed into the Salvation Army.

Between 1880 and 1884, she conducted a series of successful meetings in the halls of the affluent West End of London and at various resorts in England. Her preaching became more highly regarded than her husband's. She preached and raised monies to support his work among the poor in the East End of London.

Catherine Booth campaigned hard for social issues, waging war on poverty and forced labor. Along with her daughters, she recruited and trained hundreds of working class women for the Salvation Army. She also strongly advocated the right of women to hold the same positions as men.

Booth wrote many books dealing with holiness and Christian living. She died of cancer in October 1890.

Although William Booth was referred to as the General, Catherine, because of all her labors, became known as "The Army Mother." Today more than 3 million people belong to the organization they founded, the Salvation Army. 🏵

Joseph Martin is a Pentecostal historian-researcher and is the resource director at Victory Bible Institute in Tulsa, Oklahoma. He has compiled The Spirit-Filled Woman *devotional (Charisma House) along with several other books.*

THE HOUSE THAT HOPE BUILT
by Brenda J. Davis

Sara Trollinger has established a much-needed haven for teen-agers who are battered by life's storms.

Published reports on the state of the American family often reveal problems due to parental neglect and teen-age rebellion. But House of Hope, an outreach to teens and their families based in Orlando, Florida, has become a national model for ministries seeking to bring about family recovery and reconciliation.

Sara Trollinger, founder and president of House of Hope, was a schoolteacher for 25 years. Because of her work with emotionally handicapped students, she sometimes conducted classes with troubled teen-agers who were behind bars.

She saw countless young people bound by destructive behavior patterns. Many of them appeared to be hopelessly stuck in the public reform system.

"The same young people would come and go without any lasting help because we weren't allowed to mention the name of Jesus Christ," Sara says. "It was like a revolving door."

She began praying for a way to make a difference, and in 1985 God gave her the vision for a nondenominational residential treatment facility where troubled teen-agers could receive counseling for life-controlling issues, be taught Christian principles and see the love of God in action.

Soliciting the prayer efforts of five others, Sara trusted God for opportunities to move the vision forward. When an affordable property became available, the group took the $200 they had between them and made a down payment on what would become the ministry's first home.

Believing that God would supply the additional $95,000 she needed, Sara applied for a grant from the Edyth Bush Foundation. She was told that her chances of getting it were slim, but a single check from them covered the costs for closing on the property, and Sara's down payment of $200 was returned to her.

During House of Hope's first year an article on Sara's work appeared in a local newspaper on the same day that President Ronald Reagan was paying a visit to the city. The president read the article and wrote out a personal check to House of Hope for $1,000.

The following day, the Orlando Sentinel carried a report on how a local fledgling ministry to teen-agers had touched the heart of the chief executive. Soon the phones began ringing off their hooks.

◈ Faithfulness in Small Things

"We started out with lots of volunteers, one staff member and a part-time secretary," Sara says. "I'd work all day at school and then come back at 3 o'clock and work until midnight. I cut shrubbery. I helped wash dishes, cooked—whatever needed to be done, we'd all pitch in and do it."

As the vision became reality, Sara developed the home's procedures manual, combining the knowledge she'd gained as a teacher with godly principles she knew young people would need. She also prayed. Today the home stands as a model for 26 programs across the nation, and plans are being considered for establishing centers overseas.

Sara has come a long way from her hometown of Asheboro, North Carolina, and her dreams of being an educator. But this really isn't a major departure from what she thought her life would be.

Says Sara: "I came from a Christian family who loved the Lord. They always instilled in me that God would be as big in my life as I allowed Him to be."

Her grandmother prayed that Sara and all her siblings would go into ministry. In a sense, Sara is continuing the tradition— calling forth the destiny of the teens she helps.

Every week she teaches a class on faith. She also holds weekly "Fireside Chats," in which she meets with the groups of male and female residents separately for an hour.

"I teach every boy and girl [who] comes here that God has really specifically picked them out for such a time as this," she says.

"They are the ones who are going to lead their friends. And I believe that we are just on the brink of a great breakthrough with our young people."

❧ Getting Teens Back on Course

House of Hope accepts both Christian and non-Christian teens, ages 12 to 17. The average stay is nine months to a year and a half. Typically, by the time they leave, the residents are all born again—and most are Spirit-filled.

Young people find their way to House of Hope due to the intervention of parents and churches and sometimes at the mandate of the judicial system. Apparently, the court has no problem with the program's decidedly Christian, Spirit-filled approach—and for good reason.

"We have a 95 percent success rate for restoring teenss back to their families," Sara says. "The parents are so desperate when they come here, they'll sign papers, anything."

What parents must agree to are weekly counseling sessions, parenting classes and visits with their teen. Otherwise, they forfeit his or her participation in the program. Ongoing counseling support is available for the family once the teen goes home.

The program is founded entirely on Christian principles, but the gospel is "caught" rather than forced on anyone. Sometimes the change is so dramatic that the teen-ager will become the catalyst for the parents' conversion or rededication to live for God fully.

While in treatment the 25 boys and 25 girls attend classes in the Accelerated Christian Education program (ACE), an approved, self-paced curriculum. They can earn a high school diploma or junior college credits.

Teens are assigned a routine of counseling, worship, devotions and household duties. Many of the "toughest cases" have already been through several other programs, but "if you ask the teen-agers here what's different about this program, they'll say it's the love of God," says Sara, who credits her 30 team members for making that a reality.

❧ *Depending on God*

"I have the best staff of any place in the world. They are sold out to the Lord," she says. "When I hire somebody to come on staff I always tell them we're a faith ministry, and we may not be paid next month, but we trust in God." To date, no one has ever missed getting paid.

The ministry has chosen to forgo government funding in favor of donations and grants. Families of residents pay a portion of the costs necessary for long-term treatment. The amount is based on what they can afford.

"We've decided we're going to depend on God," Sara says. "We don't ever know where the money's coming from. We don't have pledges. It's exciting when you can see that God is always faithful."

As a visionary leader, Sara Trollinger has had to endure criticism, but she de-emphasizes those times because the Lord always attended her obedience with healings and deliverances. Sara says, "You just file that away in light of these kinds of miracles."

Sara encourages other women who desire to make a difference to pursue God's purposes earnestly, to gain all the knowledge they can and to find like-minded people to agree with them in prayer. She says: "God will, in His perfect time, raise you up. He will be as big in your life as you allow Him to be." ❀

 Brenda Davis is editor of SpiritLed Woman. *Sara Trollinger may be reached at House of Hope, P.O. Box 560484, Orlando, FL 32856 or online at www.christianlife.com/houseofhope.*

Restore Your Soul

He restores my soul. He guides me in paths of righteousness for his name's sake.

Psalm 23:3

YOU ARE MORE THAN A CONQUEROR
by Joyce Meyer

So many Christians today complain about being victims. Wouldn't you rather be a victor?

Are you hurting? If you are, you know that physical, emotional or mental pain can make life very unpleasant. I learned this fact firsthand: I was sexually, physically, verbally and emotionally abused from the time I can remember until I left home at the age of 18. Shortly after, I was married—and during the next five years I experienced further rejection, abandonment, betrayal, and finally, divorce.

I know what it is to be a victim. But I have learned from experience and the Word of God that we can have victory over pain instead of being the victims of it. I also know that we can increase or decrease the intensity of our pain by the way we handle it.

The medical field offers "pain management" classes for people who have chronic pain that medication cannot alleviate. "Stress management" seminars are available to people who suffer from stress, which can cause emotional or mental pain as well as physical illness.

Like secular organizations developed for this purpose, the Bible also teaches "pain and stress management." Romans 8:37 says, "Yet amid all these things we are more than conquerors and gain a surpassing victory through Him who loved us" (THE AMPLIFIED BIBLE).

The key is that the victory is "through Him." If we can learn how to lean on God and receive the strength we need, we truly can "do all things through Christ who strengthens us" as stated in Philippians 4:13 (NKJV).

God is more than enough for any situation. He is El Shaddai, the all-sufficient God. As we learn to draw the needed strength from Him, we can live from strength to strength instead of from weakness to weakness. When something drains our strength and we find ourselves in a stressed or weakened position, God has promised to enable us and be our helper.

In fact, He sent the Holy Spirit expressly for this purpose. Jesus told His disciples before He died that His going away would be good for them because He would send the Holy Spirit to be their "Comforter (Counselor, Helper, Advocate, Intercessor, Strengthener, Standby)" *(John 16:7, The Amplified Bible)*.

In His earthly body, Jesus could not be with everybody all the time, helping with specific situations, but the Holy Spirit can. He is not only with the believer, but also in him. God is referred to in Scripture as "our refuge and strength, a very present help in trouble" *(Ps. 46:1, NKJV)*. We can receive His help, however, only by asking for it—by relying on and trusting in Him.

As we spend time with Him and talk with Him in a simple, familiar way—we begin to draw strength from Him. If this practice continues not only in times of weakness but also during times when we are strong, we can begin to live from strength to strength.

If we wait until we are weak to draw upon His strength, we will live from weakness to strength and back to weakness. But if we never allow our "tank to get empty," so to speak, we can live from strength to strength and from glory to glory.

What Constitutes Victory? Some people are under the misconception that victory is the absence of problems. But I don't believe that real victory is defined as "being problem-free." True victory for the child of God comes right in the midst of the storm—when it's raging and there is yet peace, when tragedy has struck and one can nevertheless say, "It is well with my soul."

Romans 8:37 says that "we are more than conquerors." I believe this means that we can have assurance of victory even before the battle begins. We can have such confidence in God that no matter what happens or threatens to happen, we can be on top rather than on the bottom. We do not have to live perpetually under something—under attack, under guilt, under financial pressure and so on.

Are you under attack or on the attack? Some people get defeated just thinking about what could happen. They continually live in fear of some future disaster.

🐦 *From Victim to Victor*

Trials will come; the Bible assures us of that *(SEE JOHN 16:33)*. But we don't have to let them get the best of us. There are several steps we can take toward becoming a victor over our situations.

🐦 Develop the proper attitude. A large part of successful pain management is developing the proper attitude toward it. I went through a period of many months during which I had almost continual headaches. I prayed and sought medical counsel, and the doctor's report was that unless I wanted to live on addictive pain medication, I would have to learn to live with and manage the headache pain.

Thankfully, his report was not the final word on the matter; God ultimately delivered me from the headaches. But during the time of trial, I learned some valuable lessons about pain management that may be applied to emotional and mental pain as well as physical.

I learned that I had to lean on God to strengthen me. Ephesians 3:16 teaches us to be strengthened in the inner man. If we are strong inside, the things coming against us from the outside cannot defeat us.

First John 4:4 says, "Greater is he that is in [me], than he that is in the world" *(KJV)*. We might say it like this, "Greater is He that is in me, than he that is coming against me."

If you are physically weak, you might need to eat to gain strength. If you are weak in faith, you undoubtedly need to eat spiritual food. Spend time in the Word and time with God in worship and fellowship, and you will experience His strength flowing into you.

I learned not to talk about the problem or even think about it unless absolutely necessary. This is a challenge because the flesh wants sympathy. Even though talking about it does not solve the problem, there is a longing in us for people to know what we are going through. Ultimately, we must learn to go to the Comforter.

The more we talk about our problems, the bigger they become. We can blow them entirely out of proportion by giving them too much attention. I learned that by paying excessive attention to my problems, I was actually paying attention to the devil.

I am not suggesting that we stick our heads in the sand like ostriches and pretend that we have no problems. I am suggesting that after doing what we can, we cast our cares on God—giving them to Him who is more than enough for any problem that ever existed.

❧ Trust God to change you. We must turn ourselves over to God and trust Him to do what we cannot. We can exercise a certain amount of discipline and self-control, but no matter how much we struggle, we cannot change ourselves. God has to do it. Otherwise, He wouldn't get the glory.

When I detect weaknesses in myself, I remember that His strength will be made perfect in them if I trust Him. God is more than enough—even to handle us!

We sometimes think God is surprised at the way we act and the things we do. We must remember that He knew us before we knew Him, and He knew everything we had ever done or ever would do. Psalm 139 says He knows even the words in our mouths that are still unuttered *(SEE V. 4)!*

I am no surprise to God, and neither are you. No matter how deep in the pit a person may find himself, God's arm is not too short to save him. We cannot uphold ourselves and cause ourselves to be able to stand in His presence. But Romans 14:4 says, "And he shall stand and be upheld, for the Master—the Lord—is mighty to support him and make him stand" *(THE AMPLIFIED BIBLE).*

❧ Submit yourself to God. To get from being the victim to being victorious, we must know the truth about resisting the devil. We are taught in the Word of God: Submit yourselves therefore to God. Resist the devil, and he will flee from you (James 4:7, KJV).

I believe this Scripture tells us that true resistance is found in submission. As we submit to God and His instructions, we are resisting the devil.

Satan has a plan for our destruction, but God has a plan of deliverance and victory—a plan to prosper us and not to harm us *(SEE JER. 29:11).* It is His will that His children be victors, not victims.

To experience the victory, we must follow His instructions.

The book of James teaches us that when we are experiencing trials of any sort and are deficient in wisdom, we are to ask God, who will give to us liberally and ungrudgingly, without reproach (SEE JAMES 1:5). In other words, He will show us what to do or what not to do in order to have victory. Then we must draw strength from Him, and do it by His grace.

I thought for years that resisting the devil meant only that I should take some sort of determined stand against him. I believed if I rebuked him long enough and loud enough, he would eventually leave me alone.

However, I discovered this was not the case. When I finally sought God for answers to my own weaknesses and lack of victory over them, I realized that though I was attempting to resist the devil, I was not submitting myself to God and His instructions. God will show us how to get out of trouble, but we must pay heed to His advice and take action as He leads.

For example, the answer to your pain, if it is caused by stress, may be declining some of the opportunities for service or social activities that come your way and thus reducing the demands on your time. Learn to say no! The person who refuses to minimize the number of items on his schedule at the direction of the Holy Spirit will continue to suffer the effects of stress no matter how long and hard he resists the devil.

Many times I was so upset by my approach to the problems of life that I ended up acting like the devil instead of resisting him. Many Christians are not very nice when they are having personal problems. Our response to the storm partially determines the length of the storm. We can learn to manage our pain and not let the devil manage us.

❧ Persevere. Remember: This too shall pass! What you're going through won't last forever, but God will...and so will you. The Bible teaches us to endure. We might say that means "to outlast the devil."

Paul wrote to the Hebrews, "You need to persevere so that when you have done the will of God, you will receive what He has promised" *(HEB. 10:36, NIV)*. He reminded them that their hope in God was not in vain, "for He who promised is faithful," and that their confidence in Him would be richly rewarded *(vv. 23,35)*. Paul's counsel applies to us today. Let us declare with him, "We are not of those who shrink back and are destroyed, but of those who believe and are saved" *(v. 39)*.

I could easily have given up when I was overwhelmed by the emotional pain that came from many years of rejection and abuse. Even the healing process the Holy Spirit took me through brought fresh anguish as He led me to deal with issues from my past. But I was determined to be free, and I learned to trust God to deliver me—in His timing—and to turn my sorrow into joy *(SEE PS. 30:5; 126:5)*.

If you, too, are determined to be free—to be more than a conqueror—remember to keep your eyes and your conversation on Jesus and off the situation. Submit yourself to God in all things. Spend quality time with the Lord, drawing upon His strength. Wait in His presence, and you will find that He is more than enough to bring you through to victory, no matter what kind of pain you may be experiencing. ❀

Joyce Meyer is founder and president of Life in the Word, Inc. She travels extensively conducting conferences and speaking at local churches. She also ministers regularly via Life in the Word radio and television broadcasts.

FOR FURTHER STUDY ON THIS TOPIC:

BEAUTY FOR ASHES
BY JOYCE MEYER (WARNER FAITH)

WOMAN, THOU ART LOOSED!
BY T.D. JAKES (ALBURY)

DANCING IN THE ARMS OF GOD
BY CONNIE NEAL (ZONDERVAN)

GOD TRUSTED MARY... CAN HE TRUST YOU?

by T.D. Jakes

When God gave Mary an incredible promise, she was willing to believe and obey—even when her promised Son went to the cross.

What does a man look for in a woman? The answer may surprise you. Initially he may be attracted by looks, a certain style, a winning personality. But when it comes to making a commitment, the main issue for men is trust. It is much easier for a man to give his body than to give his heart. Before he commits his heart to a woman, he must know: Can I trust you?

What does God look for in a woman? When He has an extraordinary work that needs to be done, when He has a special calling that requires a "certain someone," how does He choose? Again, the issue is trust.

Consider Mary, the young woman selected by God to birth His only begotten Son. What was it about Mary that persuaded God to choose her? The Bible tells us nothing about her appearance—nothing about her hair, her stature, her shape, the texture of her skin or even the attractiveness of her personality. Yet according to the angel who greeted her, she was "highly favored" and "blessed...among women" *(LUKE 1:28, NKJV)*.

Why was she chosen? I believe the answer can be found on the lips of Simeon, the old man in the temple who took the baby Jesus in his arms, blessed God and spoke these words to Mary: "Behold, this Child is destined for the fall and rising of many in Israel, and for a sign which will be spoken against (yes, a sword will pierce through your own soul also), that the thoughts of many hearts may be revealed" *(LUKE 2:34-35, EMPHASIS ADDED)*.

I believe God chose Mary because He knew He could trust her. And not just with good times. Anyone can do well when times are good, when blessing and prosperity and comfort are the norm.

He knew He could trust her with trouble! Throughout her life her heart would be pierced, again and again. Yet Mary could be counted on, in the words of the commercial, to "take a lickin' and keep on tickin'."

The fact is, when you've been selected by God, it's for the long haul. His question is not "Can I trust you for one event?"; it's "Can I trust you through stages and ages, through eras and eons, to be as faithful at the end of time as you were at the beginning?

"Can I trust you to go through changes and still not change? Can I trust you to relocate and never move? Can I trust you to be altered and never be different?"

Simeon told Mary that a sword would pierce her soul. She was about to embark on a journey into the very purpose of her life—and it would cost her everything.

"For the word of God is living and powerful, and sharper than any two-edged sword, piercing even to the division of soul and spirit, and of joints and marrow" (HEB. 4:12). If you are going to find God's word for you—if you are going to fulfill His will and purpose for your life—I guarantee the journey will pierce your soul as it did Mary's.

Can He trust you? Can you be counted on to "deliver," even though your heart is pierced in the process?

Mary's heart went through seven "piercings"—seven painful trials, seven tests of trust—that might have shaken and moved any one of us. But in them all, Mary proved that God's trust in her had not been misplaced.

You, too, will suffer many piercings if you're serious about pursuing the will of God for your life. But you can learn from Mary's example as you face the questions that are on God's heart:

❧ Can He trust you with misunderstanding? Not even Joseph understood at first. All he knew was that he was engaged to a young girl carrying a baby she said God gave her! God straightened him out, but Mary still faced the whispers and sneers of the other people around her. She walked through adversity and delivered in the midst of misunderstanding—without fighting for herself or arguing to prove it was a holy thing.

God never has to be defended. And when He has called you to get the job done, you can be confident that"He who has begun a good work in you will complete it until the day of Jesus Christ" (*PHIL. 1:6*).

If you are going to be"highly favored,"if God is going to do anything mighty in your life, you cannot spend all your time trying to get everybody to understand and agree with you. Are you willing to be controversial to produce the"Christ"in you? Is God doing something important enough in your spirit for you to endure misunderstanding?

  Can He trust you to hide the treasure? Mary took the wonderful baby she had birthed—the very Son of God—and hid her"treasure"for two years in Egypt. God knew that He could trust her to possess a great treasure—and keep it to herself.

Can God trust you to keep a secret? Can He do something wonderful in your life, knowing you will not flaunt it? Can He give you an ability, knowing you will not rush to put it on stage?

The birth of Jesus was a new thing. It had never happened before! Some of the things God wants to do in your life will be new, as well. But like Mary, you have to know when to hide the "new thing."

Mary took Jesus to Egypt to escape Herod's death warrant. The enemy is after your"baby,"too. He is after your dream, your vision. He wants to kill it early, before it is fully developed.

Just as God had to know that He could trust Mary with a supernatural blessing, that He could depend on her to hide it until the time was right, He wants to know: Can He trust you to hide the treasure He's given you until the appointed time?

  Can He trust you through separation? When Mary and Joseph left Jerusalem for Nazareth after the Passover, they realized that 12-year-old Jesus had been left behind. Distraught, Mary returned to the temple to retrieve Him.

"Why did you seek Me?"responded Jesus, who had been amazing the teachers with his wisdom."Did you not know that I must be about My Father's business?" (*LUKE 2:49*).

At that point, Mary had to be willing to go home alone, separated from the precious Son she had birthed and raised. Like Mary, you may not always be able to maintain a relationship with the person or thing you are attached to. After all, this is not about you; this is for God's glory!

God needs to know that when He gives you something special, you will give it back to Him and remain separated from it—even though you care about it. Can God trust you to say, "I love you, Lord," even through separation from that special person or thing?

~ Can He trust you to wait for the right timing? If Mary had one trouble, it was with timing. At the wedding in Cana, she came to Jesus and told Him the host had run out of wine. He answered, "Woman, what does your concern have to do with Me? My hour has not yet come" (JOHN 2:4).

Timing is so important! If you are going to be successful in dance, you must be able to respond to rhythm and timing. It's the same in the Spirit.

People who don't understand God's timing can become spiritually spastic, trying to make the right things happen at the wrong time. They don't get His rhythm—and everyone can tell they are out of step. They birth things prematurely, threatening the very lives of their God-given dreams.

There is a time for everything. Can God trust you to resist pressure that would rush you into His plan for your life?

~ Can He trust you with rejection? Once, when Jesus was teaching a crowd, Mary came to see him. But when Jesus' disciples told Him she was waiting outside, He responded, "Who is My mother and who are My brothers?" Pointing to His disciples, He added, "Here are My mother and My brothers! For whoever does the will of My Father in heaven is My brother and sister and mother" (MATT. 12:48-50).

Jesus' own mother—the woman who went through pain, endured scandal, and nurtured and protected Him all His life—had to face rejection. You, too, will be rejected.

You won't always get the answer you want from God. People won't always respond to you or your ministry the way you'd like. Can you be trusted to remain faithful?

What do you do when you've danced all over the church and

you're still not healed? What do you do when you get "slain in the Spirit" and the debt is still there? What do you do when you pray the seven-step prayer and the crisis doesn't go away? Can God say "no" and trust that you will still dance, still pray, still praise Him?

❧ Can He trust you through death? At Golgotha, Mary watched her Son hang from a wretched, rugged cross—watched everything that she had labored for, fought for and built her life around—die. And yet she never turned her head. She never walked away, even though her whole world was falling apart.

Can God trust you through trauma and death—the death of a dream, of something you built your whole life around?

What do you do when things don't turn out as you thought they would? What do you when being in God's will breaks your heart?

Mary stood at the base of the cross and said, like Job, "Though He slay me, yet will I trust Him" (JOB 13:15). She could not have understood what was happening.

She did not know that through her Son's death, God was reconciling the world to Himself. She had no idea that in three days, He would be resurrected to new life. She just stood there watching, trusting a God she didn't understand.

When God's purpose brings pain in your life, can you be trusted to stand and say, "God, You can still count on me"?

❧ Can He trust you through disappointment? After Jesus' death Mary walked away from Golgotha, but she did not walk away from God. The Scriptures say that she was still part of the church. She was at all the services. She was still worshiping and praising God, raising her hands, saying, "God, You're good! I magnify You. I worship You. I adore You."

Mary kept going. She was in the upper room on the day of Pentecost when "suddenly there came a sound from heaven, as of a rushing mighty wind" (ACTS 2:2).

The Bible says that everyone in the room was filled with the Holy Spirit. But Mary had a unique distinction: This was not a new experience for her! When the Holy Spirit filled her, she knew who it was because He had filled her once before.

Have you experienced the piercings that Mary did? Are you

someone who has survived hell and high water and still says, "I love you, God. Your will be done"? Are you able to praise Him not only through the good times but also when everything is going wrong? When you don't understand?

God wants to bless you with favor and victory. He wants to birth great things in and through you. He wants you to know His resurrection power.

But the Scripture is clear: If you want to know Jesus and "the power of His resurrection," you must be willing to enter into "the fellowship of His sufferings" (PHIL. 3:10). God is still looking for women like Mary—women He can trust with trouble. Can He trust you? 🌸

Bishop T.D. Jakes is founder and pastor of the Potter's House Church in Dallas, Texas. He is also the author of several books, including Daddy Loves His Girls *and* Woman, Thou Art Loosed!

FOR FURTHER STUDY ON THIS TOPIC:

HOLY BIBLE, WOMAN THOU ART LOOSED EDITION
T.D. JAKES, GENERAL EDITOR (THOMAS NELSON)

A WOMAN GOD CAN LEAD
BY ALICE MATHEWS (DISCOVERY HOUSE)

NAMES OF WOMEN OF THE BIBLE
BY JULIE-ALLYSON IERON (MOODY)

BERTHA SMITH
by Lewis and Betty Drummond

FORERUNNERS OF FAITH
Awakening China to the Gospel

Bertha Smith was born on Nov. 16, 1888, on a farm outside Cowpens, South Carolina. She was one of five children of John and Frances Smith.

A disciplined, precocious child, she had a dynamic conversion experience and came to Jesus Christ during a Baptist revival meeting in 1905.

While in college in 1910, Bertha realized that God wanted her to become a missionary. Then in 1917, she received her formal appointment to China from the Southern Baptist's International Mission Board (formerly Foreign Mission Board).

After a year of language study in Peking (now Beijing), "Miss Bertha," as she was affectionately called, went to her first assignment in Laichowfu, in Shantung province. She developed a burden for the Chinese Christians to whom she ministered and the millions of Chinese people who had not yet come to faith in Christ.

Apathy pervaded the churches in Shantung, but a time of political upheaval caused the missionaries there to retreat to the seaport city of Chefoo, where an unforgettable event took place.

During a prayer meeting there were dramatic healings, reconciliations and salvations. But Bertha disciplined the group for their half-hearted commitment toward the people they had been sent to help.

The revived missionaries returned to their respective stations as different people with a different message. Now they were ready to minister in power. And they did.

The great Shantung Revival began in 1927 and continued until the Japanese invasion in 1936. The awakening deepened and spread to other areas.

There was deep conviction among Chinese Christian leaders and missionaries alike. Physical healings were verified, and thousands found Christ.

Bertha had a fruitful ministry in China until she returned to America in 1942. Seven years later she made her way to the Island of Formosa (Taiwan) where the revival continued.

At age 70 Bertha retired to America and wrote a best-selling book that told the story of the great Chinese revival. For nearly 30 years, she traveled across the world sharing one message: God revives His people. She was called home to her reward on June 12, 1988, just five months before her 100th birthday. 🏵

Lewis Drummond is a professor of Evangelism and Church Growth at Beeson Divinity School in Birmingham, Alabama. He and his wife, Betty, are the authors of several titles, including The Spiritual Woman *(Kregel Publications).*

THERE'S NO SUCH THING AS RETIREMENT

by Nancy Justice

At 80 years old, Eleanor Workman is still feeding, housing and teaching hundreds of orphans in Haiti.

Childhood is supposed to be a carefree, idyllic time, a time of making happy memories to cherish and remember throughout life. Not so for the children of Haiti, where most youngsters, even 4- and 5-year-olds, can be found carrying water jugs on their heads, baby-sitting, running errands or cleaning house. Statistics show that in this, the poorest nation in the western hemisphere, about half the children die before age 5 because of starvation, malnutrition or exposure to disease and inclement weather. Many are abandoned by their parents or orphaned and left to roam the streets, begging for food.

But amid the destitution, political upheaval, voodoo worship and witchcraft that hangs like a heavy, dark cloud over this small island in the West Indies, there is an angel by the name of Eleanor "Mom"Workman who relies on the power of God to save—both physically and spiritually—as many of Haiti's children as possible.

The energetic 5-foot-4-inch, 120-pound Eleanor is 80 years old and doesn't plan on slowing down. In the 27 years she's lived in Haiti, she's accomplished, virtually singlehandedly, what it would take most government agencies ages to do.

Her five-acre Christian Haitian Outreach (CHO) compound in Mariani, located just outside Port-au-Prince, houses an orphanage, a school, dormitories, offices, a church, a playground and a soccer field. The orphanage has been home to a total of about 1,800 children, ranging from newborns to teen-agers.

Many of the children are brought to CHO by area doctors as seemingly hopeless cases. But during daily worship, called Baby

Prayer Time, everyone from the youngest baby to the oldest adult staffer gathers together, and Eleanor teaches them how to pray and beseech God for divine healing.

In Haiti education is not mandatory, and parents who are unemployed are unable to send their children to school because they can't pay required fees or buy school uniforms. To assist such parents and their children, Eleanor fills her school—current enrollment is about 600—with the poorest of the poor.

Many graduates have gone on to college or trade school while others joined CHO's staff. One bright young man was accepted into medical school but lacked funding. Eleanor dipped into her own pension fund to pay his tuition. He is now doing his internship and plans to return to Mariani to run a much-needed medical clinic.

Eleanor first came to Mariani when she was 52—an age when most folks are slowing down in preparation for retirement. But upon seeing the rampant poverty, she soon found herself running a makeshift school under a tree in an empty lot.

"I didn't have any money or funds," says Eleanor, "but I was so concerned about these suffering children—I just began to love them. I put them under the tree and started teaching them the alphabet." Eleanor showed up each day with a lesson and whatever food she could find.

When asked to care for 6-week-old twins who had been found on a garbage dump with their terminally ill mother, she rented a house and started her orphanage.

"A doctor asked me what I was going to do for the babies—they were very ill," Eleanor recounts. "I told him about the healing power of the Great Physician, Jesus."

The doctor didn't offer much hope. But before the mother died, she signed her babies over to Eleanor. Today they're 13 years old and living happily with their adoptive family in New Jersey.

ஜ *Called by God*

Like the children of Haiti, Eleanor didn't have the happiest childhood or young adulthood. She grew up in a New Jersey home with an alcoholic father. Her mother made sure her children were in church every time the doors were open. It was there that Eleanor developed a love for singing and later got saved and filled with the Holy Ghost.

She married at age 27 to a man she met at church. "I married him not because I was in love but because he and the church elders thought we should," Eleanor says. By the time the couple moved to Los Angeles, the young bride was acquainted with her husband's unfaithfulness and violent temper.

Eleanor started fasting and praying. When her husband left to take a job back East, never offering an explanation or penny of support, Eleanor accepted it as God's intervention. Years later she found out he had died.

For income, Eleanor converted her Los Angeles home into a successful, licensed day care center. "It seemed I had been born with a skill for caring for children," she says. However, there was a still small voice speaking to Eleanor about the mission field.

Faced with financial burdens, Eleanor went on a 21-day fast that culminated with God's instructing her, she says, to sell her house. Unsure she had truly heard from God, Eleanor went on a longer fast that ended with the same instruction.

Finally, she decided to put out a fleece. "I told the Lord, 'OK, I'll let the realtor list my house, but I won't let him put up a For Sale sign. Only one person may look at it, and if that person isn't interested, then I'll know this wasn't of God. I'll know the devil is trying to trick me.'"

The one person who looked at Eleanor's home decided to buy it.

Eventually Eleanor met missionaries from Haiti who invited her to come and see their work. The experience changed her life. "It made me want to give my whole life to sharing the gospel with these people," she says.

Today, when Eleanor is not in Haiti, she is traveling around North America, speaking and singing at churches and groups to raise funds for her ministry.

She leaves the CHO compound in good hands, employing 113 staffers: nine laundresses, plus teachers, nurses, cooks, housekeepers, janitors, guards, electricians, carpenters and painters.

"The children have great constant care," says Eleanor. "I've hired my neighbors. They're very happy to be here since there are no other jobs in the area."

Some may say Eleanor stands against insurmountable odds, but she fights the problems in Haiti with all she's got: prayer. "There is no defeat in the Lord Jesus Christ," she says. "I don't have money, but I have a wonderful faith. My greatest joy is to see these precious children grow up and become such vital members of God's kingdom." 🌸

 Nancy Justice is a free-lance writer in Oviedo, Florida. For more information on Eleanor Workman's ministry, write Christian Haitian Outreach, P.O. Box 634545, Margate, FL 33063-4545; or call (954) 972-3674.

WHEN YOU CAN'T FORGIVE YOURSELF
by R.T. Kendall

In Christ there is atonement for our sins. Yet we can still be tempted to keep a running tally of all we've done.

First Corinthians 13, the great love chapter of the Bible, is a perfect demonstration of the cause and effect of total forgiveness. The apex of this wonderful passage is the phrase found in verse 5, Love "keeps no record of wrongs" *(NIV)*.

The Greek word that is translated as "no record" is logizomai, which means not to reckon or impute. The word is important to Paul's doctrine of justification by faith.

For the person who believes, his faith is "credited" to him as righteousness *(SEE ROM. 4:5)*. This is the same word used in 1 Corinthians 13:5.

Therefore, not to reckon, impute or "count" the wrongs of a loved one is to do for that person what God does for us, namely, choose not to recognize his sin.

In the same way, forgiving oneself means to experience the love that keeps no record of our own wrongs. It is one thing to have this breakthrough regarding others; it is quite another to experience the greater breakthrough—total forgiveness of ourselves.

So many Christians say: "I can forgive others, but how can I ever forget what I have done? I know God forgives me, but I can't forgive myself."

We must remember that forgiving ourselves is a lifelong commitment. In precisely the same way that I must forgive others every single day, I must also forgive myself *(SEE LUKE 6:37)*.

☙ The Process of Forgiving

We must renew our commitment to forgive others each and every day for the wrongs done to us. Forgiving ourselves is also a daily process.

We may wake up each day with the awareness of past failures. We may have feelings of guilt—or pseudo-guilt, if our sins have been placed under the blood of Christ.

But forgiving yourself may bring about the breakthrough you have been looking for. It could set you free in ways you have never before experienced.

Sometimes we are afraid to forgive ourselves. We cling to fear as if it were a thing of value. The truth is, the very breath of Satan is behind the fear of forgiving ourselves.

Jesus knows that many of us have this problem. This is a further reason Jesus turned up unexpectedly after His Resurrection in the room where the disciples were assembled both in terror and in guilt.

Jesus wanted them to know they were totally forgiven; He also wanted them to forgive themselves. He spoke to them as if nothing had happened (SEE JOHN 20:21). This gave them dignity and showed them that nothing had occurred that would change Jesus' plans and strategy for them.

I remember one Sunday just before I was to preach at the 11 a.m. service. I had an argument with my wife, Louise, and stormed out of the house, slamming the door in her face.

Before I knew it, I was bowing my head on the upper platform at Westminster Chapel before several hundred people. I was thinking: I should not be here. I have no right to be here. Lord, how on Earth could You use me today? I am not fit to be in this pulpit.

There was no way to resolve the situation at that time. I could only ask God for mercy and try my best to forgive myself. Never in my life had I felt so unworthy.

But when I stood up to preach, God simply undergirded me and enabled me to preach as well as I ever had! When we are emptied of all self-righteousness and pride, we enable God to move in and through us.

֍ Why We CAN'T Forgive Ourselves

At the end of the day, I believe there are several causes for our inability to forgive ourselves.

Anger. We may be angry with ourselves. Look at the Old Testament story of Joseph. As a type of Christ, Joseph said to his brothers, "'And now, do not be distressed and do not be angry with yourselves for selling me here, because it was to save lives that God sent me ahead of you'" (Gen. 45:5).

These brothers were beginning to get the message that Joseph had forgiven them; he didn't want them to be angry with themselves. That is the way God forgives. Jesus does not want us to be angry with ourselves for our sins.

Not forgiving ourselves is self-hatred. Joseph's brothers had hated themselves for selling Joseph into slavery. They could not take back what they had done.

Some Christians who can't forgive themselves are, underneath it all, angry with themselves. But God can begin today to cause all that happened to fit into a pattern for good.

God will take the wasted years and restore them to good before it is all over. It is just as Joel promised: "I will repay you for the years the locusts have eaten" (Joel 2:25).

In some cases it is fear more than anger that is a barrier to our forgiving ourselves. Regret leads to guilt, and guilt can lead to fear: the fear of missing "what might have been" or the fear that what has happened cannot possibly turn out for good.

True guilt and pseudo-guilt. There are two kinds of guilt most of us will struggle with: true guilt (a result of our sin against God) and pseudo-guilt (when there is no sin in our lives). When we have sinned, we must confess it to God (see 1 John 1:9). The blood of Jesus takes care of true guilt by doing two basic things:

- ❧ It washes away our sin—as though it never had existed.
- ❧ It perfectly satisfies God's eternal justice.

Whereas discipline is necessary because we are sinners, sin that has been confessed to God is totally forgiven by Him. Any guilt we feel after that is pseudo-guilt.

There are two kinds of false guilt:

- ❧ The kind that comes when sin was never involved in the first place.

~ The kind that comes when sin has been forgiven by God.

Pseudo-guilt—though it is false—is also very real; we feel keenly guilty. But there is no good reason for the sense of guilt.

Take, for example, a person who is driving a car when a child runs out into the street at the last second and is struck down. The guilt can be overwhelming, but there was no sin. It doesn't need to be confessed to God.

The other kind of pseudo-guilt comes when you have confessed your sins but you don't feel forgiven. Once we have acknowledged our sin, we should accept our forgiveness and leave the rest in God's hands.

During the years I have developed a sense of failure as a father. I wish I had given more time to T.R. and Melissa in my early years at Westminster Chapel.

I now understand that putting them first—rather than my church or sermon preparation—would have allowed the Chapel to carry on just as well. Of course, I can't change the past.

But for me to continue to feel guilty over this is not pleasing to God because He has already totally forgiven me. If I let myself dwell on my failure, I am giving in to pseudo-guilt and sinning as I do because I am dignifying unbelief. I must keep destroying the record of my wrongs—every day.

Not forgiving ourselves is a subtle way of competing with Christ's atonement. God has already punished Jesus for what we did (SEE 2 COR. 5:17). Instead of accepting Jesus' sacrifice, I want to punish myself for my failures. This competes with Christ's finest hour.

Fear. Fear is one of the main reasons we do not forgive ourselves. The person who fears has not been made perfect in love, and fear "has to do with punishment" (1 JOHN 4:18).

Recognizing that fear—and punishing ourselves for our mistakes—displeases God should result in an ever-increasing sadness for this self-loathing spirit. We are required to walk away from our past folly and not look back.

My wife was greatly blessed by the music ministry of Janny Grein and her song "Movin' On" at a Rodney Howard-Browne meeting. Louise remembers Janny shouting out the words: "Let the past be past—at last." God speaks those words to us.

Let the past be past at last. Forgive yourself as well as those who have damaged you.

Pride, Self-righteousness and Self-pity. Our unforgiveness of ourselves may be traceable to pride. We, in our arrogance, cannot bear having the Lord do everything for us so graciously, so we think we must help Him out a bit.

Our pride must be eclipsed by humility. We must let God be God and the blood of Christ do what it in fact did: remove our guilt and satisfy God's sense of justice.

Just as fear and pride are like identical twins, so are self-righteousness and self-pity. We feel sorry for ourselves and show it by not forgiving ourselves.

Pseudo-guilt can develop into very real guilt before God. It is false guilt, since God says, "You're not guilty." We make it into real guilt when we in effect reply, "Yes, I am."

The bottom line is this: Not forgiving ourselves is wrong and dishonoring to God. But God will use the sorrow we feel over what we've done to draw us to Himself.

Guilt and Grace. The initial work of the Holy Spirit is that He convicts of sin. When we walk in the light we know the blood cleanses us of sin, but walking in the light also reveals sin in us that we may not have seen before *(SEE 1 JOHN 1:7-8)*.

The sense of guilt God instigates is temporary. God uses guilt only to get our attention. When we say, "I'm sorry," and mean it, that's enough for God.

He doesn't beat us black and blue and require us to go on a 30-day fast to supplement Christ's atonement. He convicts us of sin to get our attention, but having done that, He wants us to move forward.

The ability to forgive ourselves therefore extends from an understanding of grace. Grace is undeserved favor.

Mercy is not getting what we do deserve (justice). Grace is accepting what we don't deserve (total forgiveness).

It may seem unfair when we have been so horrible. We have let God down; we have let others down.

But it is fair *(SEE 1 JOHN 1:9)*. The blood of Jesus did a wonderful job. God is not looking for further satisfaction.

All accusations regarding confessed sin come from the devil, who works either as a roaring lion to scare or an angel of light to deceive—or both *(SEE 1 PET. 5:8; 2 COR. 11:14)*. Never forget, perfect love drives out fear *(SEE 1 JOHN 4:18)*.

☙ *Let the Past Be Past*

The sweet consequence of not keeping a record of all wrongs is that we let go of the past and its effect on the present. We cast our care on God and rely on Him to restore the wasted years and to cause everything to turn out for good.

We find ourselves accepting ourselves as we are with all our failures (just as God does), knowing all the while our potential to make more mistakes. God never becomes disillusioned with us; He loves us and knows us inside out.

Moses, David, Jonah, Peter—all these men in the Bible had to forgive themselves before they could move into the ministry God had planned for them. It's time for you to follow their example.

That is exactly what God wants of you and me. Let the past be past—at last. ❀

 R.T. Kendall is the author of Total Forgiveness, *published by Charisma House, from which this article is adapted.*

FOR FURTHER STUDY ON THIS TOPIC:

TOTAL FORGIVENESS
BY R.T. KENDALL (CHARISMA HOUSE)

THE GIFT OF FORGIVENESS
BY CHARLES STANLEY (THOMAS NELSON)

BREAKING FREE
BY BETH MOORE (BROADMAN & HOLMAN)

NEVERTHELESS, GOD REMEMBERS

by Mark Rutland

Our earthly sense of fairness isn't always in sync with God's ways. But be assured, God never wastes His servants, nor will He forget their suffering.

Blind and frail, her wiry, white hair stirred ever so slightly by a faint, hot breeze, the old German missionary came slowly toward me. She could not possibly have known I was there with two Africans, watching her tap her way slowly across the baked, grassless "lawn" of the guesthouse.

"Who is she?" I asked.

"Bible translator. Now she has river blindness."

"She will die?"

"Yes. She will die. She is going back to Germany. She will die there."

"What did she do here?" I asked.

"She put the Bible into two languages."

"All by herself?"

"All by herself."

"Now she goes home to die in Germany."

"All by herself."

The unfairness—the lonely, blind, painful unfairness of it—swamped me. I stood there slowly sinking into a bottomless marsh of injustice.

She should have been on a dais at a head table, receiving honors and applause and the undying gratitude of thousands. A sightless Lufthansa flight and a few months unvisited in a ward where impoverished old ladies die seemed the wrong ending for a holy life full of great kingdom accomplishments.

Then, as though I could hear her thoughts—or were they God's?—I seemed to find relief, even joy, in Paul's words, "For the which cause I also suffer these things: nevertheless I am not ashamed: for I know whom I have believed, and am persuaded that He is able to keep that which I have committed unto Him against that day" *(2 TIM. 1:12, KJV).*

❧ God's Ways Are Not Our Ways

The Bible nowhere promises Christ's ambassadors some rose-petaled aisleway of safety through suffering. Indeed, Scriptures such as Psalm 34:19 say the exact opposite: "Many are the afflictions of the righteous."

Even the most righteous among us will "suffer these things," as Paul says. However we try to impose upon God our limited human fairness doctrines, He will not submit.

In our reasoning, the mother of three must have three identical candy bars or none at all. If she has only one, it must be divided equally, with a ruler, while all three kibitz. We cannot imagine that mother standing her youngest before the other two and, without apparent merit, awarding him alone candy.

"Watch," she admonishes the two candy-bar-less siblings. "Look how your brother relishes that gooey chocolate. See the obvious delight in his eyes, the salacious way he licks his lips. Rejoice with him and be glad."

Yet that is precisely what God does. He lifts one to prominence and public blessing, plants his feet in a broad place and anoints his ministry before the eyes of the world.

Another pours out his life in the jungle, and the Peruvian Air Force shoots down his plane, killing his wife and child. Ministry, hardship, suffering, blessing, miracles, signs, wonders and unspeakable agony seem all jumbled in the fruit basket of life, which defies our cozy explanations and tidy little formulas of faith.

Only one word—"nevertheless"—will make sense of it all and bring a victorious joyful meaning to it, for that word scatters the midnight of temporal confusion with the dawn of eternal significance. Satan has practiced his arguments, learned his lines well and never misses an opportunity to plunge the dagger deep into the soft, defenseless tissue of our pain.

"You see," he says, "there is your God for you. You see how He is. He lets you work like a slave, pour out your heart, preach till you drop, pray without ceasing, and He rewards you with a church split, angry elders and rabid sheep tearing your flesh to shreds. Do you deny these facts?"

"No."

"Are you or are you not suffering?" Satan asks.

"I am."

"Well, what do you have to say to this fine mess?" he mocks.

If our wounded confusion is on one side of this grand word, what is on the other? We stand unmoved on "nevertheless."

The weight of our apparently unrewarded labors so oppressive in their density is on one side of this word. On the other rests an unchanging and unchangeable biblical truth.

☞ Nothing Will Be Lost

In 2 Timothy 1:12, Paul gives us a two-part anthem to follow his nevertheless. Either part is, by itself, wonderful; but together they are magnificent:

"I know whom I have believed," Paul says. In the midst of trial by fire, who God is remains the greater, infinitely greater truth than what is happening.

Plant your faith in the miracles of God, and you are ripe for satanic attack. Anchor your soul in the God of miracles, and circumstances can never dislodge your hope.

Whom you have believed may someday be all you have to cling to. The thing is, it will be enough.

"And am persuaded that He is able to keep that which I have committed unto Him against that day." Your life, faith and labors of love on Christ's behalf are not lost under the clutter of papers on God's disheveled desk. Regardless of what you may think just now, what you may actually hear Satan screaming in your ear, God keeps, carefully and lovingly, all that is committed into His hands.

Nothing is lost. Nothing is even temporarily mislaid. On that day, at that lovely dawn of clear bright truth, it will be right there where you put it, in His hands.

This part of the passage might well be translated top side down to read, "I know whom I have believed and am persuaded that He is able to keep that which He has committed unto me against that day."

Read that way it brings sweet assurance that God will not put any burden or any calling, responsibility or ministry in my hands that He will not keep in His. The ultimate responsibility for the outcome is not mine—but His. My responsibility is to intentionally place back in His hands all that He puts in mine.

This is not just for the dying missionary, but for all who have felt unappreciated. The mom whose daily sacrifices are so carelessly trod upon by those for whom she labors. The steady-Freddy—the lusterless, unimaginative husband and father who pays the mortgage, hits the backyard grounders and attends the PTA.

It's true for the retired executive who wonders if his former employees remember or appreciate his efforts to keep them all on the payroll through three recessions. It's true for the inner-city teacher who watches her dedicated creativity oozing its lifeblood on the floor of a dirty, gray classroom full of sneakered barbarians who care nothing about her heroic efforts to ignite some spark of life in them.

In the jeering din of demonic accusations of wastage, we can whisper the one great word that puts the enemy to flight and lights the corners of the room for all the unappreciated: "Nevertheless."

I know who my God is, and I am eternally convinced He will not let anything go unseen or unrewarded. When Satan tenderly drapes the dreary, but oh, so delicious afghan of self-pity around our slumping shoulders and begins to whisper, we need not let him even finish his sentence.

"What about all the...?"

Nevertheless.

"Who will repay all the...?"

Nevertheless.

"Look, they all forgot your..."

Nevertheless. ❀

Mark Rutland is president of Southeastern College in Lakeland, Florida, and the founder and president of Global Servants, an international missions ministry that provides training and support to national pastors and leaders. He is the author of Nevertheless *(Charisma House), from which this article is adapted.*

FOR FURTHER STUDY ON THIS TOPIC:

NEVERTHELESS
BY MARK RUTLAND (CHARISMA HOUSE)

A CHANCE TO DIE
BY ELISABETH ELLIOTT (FLEMING H. REVELL)

THE HIDING PLACE
BY CORRIE TEN BOOM (BANTAM)

THE LESSON OF THE SEED-GRAIN
by Jessie Penn-Lewis

All of us want to bear fruit for the kingdom, but the only way to bring forth life is to die.

Jesus used many analogies to teach us the truths of the kingdom. One of these was the lesson of the seed-grain, in which He compared the life of the believer to the process of development of a grain of wheat.

"'Unless a grain of wheat falls into the gound and dies,'" He said, "'it remains alone; but if it dies, it produces much grain'" (JOHN 12:24, NKJV). This process is the same one we must go through if we are to bear fruit as we are called to do.

Let us turn to the seed-grain and see the picture lesson, that in these last days we may intelligently yield to the pierced hand of God and permit His fullest purposes to be fulfilled in us.

Joined to the Lord, the grain of wheat awakens to the law of its being and yields itself to the Son of God for sowing in the earth. It cries to God to make it fruitful at any cost. The purpose of its life begins to dawn upon it. It sees that there is an element of selfishness in being absorbed in its "own" advancement and its "own" growth.

The heavenly Husband man hears the cry of the grain of wheat, prompted by the Holy Spirit, and silently begins to prepare it for the answer to its prayers. He prepares it for sowing in the ground by gently detaching it from the bands that bind it to its stalk.

It may appear as if He has not heeded the cry, and the little grain wonders why He does not answer; but the air and sunshine are doing their silent work. The grain is ripening, unconsciously to itself, until suddenly it finds itself loosened from its old ties. A hand takes hold of it, and it is dropped down into the dark earth.

♯ *Separation*

What has happened? The little grain of wheat asked for fruit, not this strange path. Where are the sunshine, the old companions, the former happy experiences?

"Where am I?" cries the lonely grain. "Where is my cozy stalk? This dark spot of earth, so repulsive, seems to be injuring my nice coat; it was so beautiful in my little nest on the top of the stalk. I was so far away from earth, so far above all." So the little grain speaks within itself.

Presently it is shocked to find its covering beginning to deteriorate. So long as it could retain its exterior beauty it did not mind the isolation, the darkness, the apparent uselessness. But this is too much.

Moreover it seems to be "giving way" to its surroundings. It is broken by them and is not able to guard itself and remain "far above all" as before. It thought it would never be moved by earthly things again.

However, in spite of these strange dealings, the little grain rests on the faithfulness of God. It knows He will lead it safely by a way that it knows not. It cries with the psalmist, "I shall yet praise Him, the help of my countenance and my God" *(Ps. 42:11)*.

♯ *Loss of Identity*

Poor little grain! Now trampled upon in the dark earth, buried out of sight, ignored, forgotten, this little grain of wheat was once greatly admired. How the other grains looked up to it and listened with reverence to its counsels!

Now it feels forgotten as it passes into solitude, crying, "I looked for someone to take pity, but there was none; and for comforters, but I found none" *(Ps. 69:20)*. It longs for other children of God who may "tell of the sorrow of those whom Thou hast wounded." But these seem to have no anguish of heart for suffering with others.

Buried grain, say "yes" to God. He is answering your prayers to become fruitful!

Maybe you were occupied with your successful service and with your happy experience in those old days. How little you were able to understand the temptations and the difficulties of the little blades of wheat. How stern you were with those who fell, not "considering yourself lest you also be tempted" (GAL. 6:1).

How you talked to the tiny blades of green just peeping through the ground, stating that they "ought" to be much older and more mature! How "weak" you thought them because they were bowed to the ground as soon as some heavy foot trod upon them.

How you discouraged them when they were weak in the faith and did not "receive them" nor bear lovingly with their weaknesses! How you tried to make them see what you saw in your greater maturity. You did not understand how to wait and to encourage them and to give them time to grow!

Buried grain, you were "truly guilty concerning [your] brother" (GEN. 42:21) in your lack of "anguish of heart and many tears" over the temptations and sorrows of others. How you guarded yourself and feared to stoop down to earth—to become as weak to the weak, that you might gain the more!

❧ Brokenness

Now learn the mystery of the kingdom unfolded in the picture lesson of the grain of wheat: The life of God in you could not break forth into fruitfulness until you had been broken by God's own hand. The earthly surroundings and testings, the loneliness and humiliation, were permitted by Him so that He might release into life abundant the life that had come from God.

At each stage of growth there must be the casting off of much that was necessary before if there is to be fuller development. At the beginning, the germ of life is hidden within the outward form of the written word; the shell may pass away (that is, from our memories) but the life—the Living Word—remains. Under favorable conditions for growth, in "an honest and good heart," cleansed from all that would choke the seed, the life progresses, showing itself in varied outward forms that may be described as the blade, the stalk, the ear, the full corn in the ear.

In the fullness of time the knife must be used, for there must come the severing from old supports, the parting with old experiences, the passing away of outward things that once helped us. The blades of green, the stalk, the ear of wheat—these were only outward coverings for a life that was pressing through them to full maturity.

Severed from old supports, detached from old surroundings, again the life within the matured grain cannot break forth into the hundredfold without a further stripping—a breaking of an outward shell that would prevent the fruitfulness.

In honest hearts crying out to God for His fullest purposes to be fulfilled in them, the Holy Spirit works even when they do not understand His working. The danger lies in their clinging to old experiences, old helps and old supports when the Spirit-life within is pressing them on to another stage—especially if that stage seems "downward" instead of "upward." Our picture lesson shows us that "downward" means fruitfulness and is the sequence to the "upward" path of the full development of the grain of wheat.

What all this means in practical experience the Holy Spirit alone can make us understand. It is sufficient for us to know enough of the principles of His working that we may learn to yield trustfully to all His dealings.

☙ Bearing Fruit

At last the grain of wheat is willing to be hidden away from the eyes of men. Willing to be trampled upon and lie in silence in some lonely corner chosen of God. Willing to appear what others would call a "failure." Willing to live in the will of God apart from glorious experiences. Willing to dwell in solitude and isolation, away from happy fellowship with other grains of wheat.

The little grain has learned something of the meaning of fellowship with Christ in His death, and now comes to pass the saying: "'Whoever loses his life for My sake will find it'" (*Matt. 16:25*).

Silently, surely, the divine life breaks forth into fruitfulness. The grain has given itself, it has parted with its "own life"; yet it still lives—lives now in the life of its Lord.

A buried seed-grain, it is content to be forgotten! For who thinks of the grain and of all the sorrow and suffering it underwent in the dark when they see the harvest field?

But the grain of wheat is satisfied because the law of its being is fulfilled. It has sunk itself and its own getting and now lives in others, not even desiring to have it known that from it the hundredfold has sprung.

So Christ Himself poured out His soul unto death that He might "see His seed" (Is. 53:10, KJV), see the travail of His soul and be satisfied (SEE v. 11) as He lives again in His redeemed ones. Thus in God's wondrous law—the law of nature repeated in the spiritual world—the first Grain of wheat, sown by God Himself, is reproduced in other grains, having the same characteristics and law of being: "'Unless a grain of wheat falls into the earth and dies, it remains by itself alone; but if it dies, it bears much fruit'" (JOHN 12:24, NASB).

☙ Life Out of Death

We have followed the little grain in its downward path into the ground to die. It has "hated its life in this world," and now its life is hid with Christ in God. While it has been consenting to the breaking and stripping in its lonely, hidden path, the divine life within it has been breaking forth in life to others and silently springing up into stronger, fuller, purer union with the ascended Lord.

This is not an easy path. Even the Lord Christ was troubled as He drew near the hour of desolation and suffering foreshadowed in Psalm 22. "'Now My soul has become troubled; and what shall I say? 'Father, save Me from this hour?' But for this purpose I came to this hour. Father, glorify Thy Name'" (JOHN 12:27-28).

The hiding of the Father's face was more than broken heart, nails and spear. Jesus knew what was to come, and He could have saved Himself—He could have spoken to His Father and had legions of angels fulfill His requests—but where then would have been the first fruits unto God and the Lamb? Nay, the Master's only prayer could be, "'Father, glorify Thy Name.'"

If we follow the Lamb where He went, if we are willing to die in order to bring forth life, there will surely come to us, as to Him, the assurance from the Father: "'I have both glorified it, and will glorify it again'" *(v. 28)*. And in the end a great reward will be given us: "'To Him who overcomes I will grant to sit with Me on My throne'" *(Rev. 3:21, NKJV)*. 🏵

 Jessie Penn-Lewis (1861-1927) was a frequent Keswick speaker whose messages proclaimed the centrality of the cross in the life and experience of the Christian. She regularly contributed to The Overcomer, *a worldwide quarterly, which she founded in 1908.*

FOR FURTHER STUDY ON THIS TOPIC:

FRUITFUL LIVING
BY JESSIE PENN-LEWIS (CHRISTIAN LITERATURE CRUSADE)

ALL IN GOD'S TIME
BY IVERNA TOMPKINS (CHARISMA HOUSE)

THE CHRISTIAN'S SECRET OF A HAPPY LIFE
BY HANNAH WHITALL SMITH (NELSON)

NOTHING SHALL HINDER US
by Amy Carmichael

Like spiritual mountaineers, we must brave the "elements"—difficult circumstances—in order to follow the path God has laid out for us.

☞ *Expose yourself to the circumstances of His choice.*

This little phrase, which has stood by many a climbing soul, seems to have been coined for a picture I have of the Matterhorn surrounded by billowing clouds. In this picture, the confusion of the skies has been so wonderfully captured that I can almost see the movement and hear the wind that rushes past. The clouds in the picture are sunlit, but I realize that, were they real, they could with awful speed cover the face of the mountain with darkness.

Mist, rain, snow—the clouds may bring them all, and the precipice falls away at our feet. "But none of these things move me; nor do I count my life dear to myself, so that I may finish my race with joy" (ACTS 20:24, NKJV)—so speaks the spiritual mountaineer.

Of course no parable, including this one, shows everything: We know that no natural-realm climber among the precipices purposely exposes himself to stormy wind or willingly walks into clouds. But spiritual mountaineers must; and at such an hour there must be "some perseverance when we are tired, some resoluteness not to let ourselves off easily," something akin to the spirit of the world's mountaineers, "a spirit firm and tenacious and ambitious enough to drive on the body to its seemingly last extremity."

There is no such thing as an easy or a sheltered climb. But "what know they of harbours who toss not on the sea?" And what know they of succor who have never ventured in difficult places? We shall press through the mist and the smothering snow; we shall climb and not give way; for there is One invisible with us, "and with every call of every hour His word is, 'Let us go hence.'"

But notice the word is "us"; we do not go alone. And we take this word in faith, just as we take such words as "The angel of the

Lord encamps all around those who fear Him, and delivers them" (Ps. 34:7), in faith.

"Therefore do not cast away your confidence, which has great reward" (HEB. 10:35). Cast it not away when Grief is a companion with whom you must become acquainted, as Jesus was. "Acquainted with grief" (Is. 53:3): The words are made real when we encounter difficult circumstances.

Two friends are bound together in love. The call to go to the foreign land for Christ comes to one but not the other. There must be renunciation then, or eternal loss.

Or something even more poignant happens. Both hear the call. One goes abroad; the other prepares to follow. But the providence of God holds that one at home. Constraint that nothing can weaken holds the other abroad.

Who can measure spiritual pain? Who can weigh the exceeding and eternal weight of glory that is being wrought while the eyes of faith are fixed, not on the pain, but on that which lies beyond it? But of this good thing they see nothing yet, not even the shadow. They know only that they will not serve their Lord together now.

Very tender comforts are prepared for such as these. They will find them as they go on.

But at least theirs is a pure sorrow. It is not touched by the soiled fingers of earth. Some find themselves in the midst of clouds and darkness because of the sinful deeds of others.

And yet the wrongdoing of another should have no power to darken the way of a child of God. At such times our peace is found in believing that things that are not good can be caused to work together for good. They are all subject to Him whose works are great and whose thoughts are deep.

This is true even when the trouble is the result of our own doing. A wrong turning was taken at the foot of the hill. A wrong decision was made that has affected the whole course of life.

The husband has been handicapped by a wife who can never enter into his deepest thoughts. The wife has been held from the highest she knew by the husband whose eyes were on the plains. Divided counsels in the bringing up of children tell upon the children.

That means sorrow.

These circumstances were not the choice of God for those lives, but it is impossible to go back and begin again, and each day will bring its trials of patience and its private griefs.

View all this as a glorious chance to prove the power of God to keep you in peace and in hope and in sweetness of spirit. In that sense "expose yourself" to those circumstances. Do not fret against them. Do not fret by a dour countenance those who cause them to be. "Beloved, let us love" *(1 JOHN 4:7)* is a wonderful word for such difficult situations. And love is happy, not dour.

Even if you seem to be pushing through some long trailing wisp of cloud, like that which lies on the face of the Matterhorn, be of good cheer. Your God has not forsaken you.

Often we find ourselves in precipitous, perhaps cloudy places because of some act of obedience. Such acts are called "ventures of faith," but there is no venture where faith is concerned. We walk on rock, not on quicksand, when we obey. But there is no promise that the rock will be a leveled path, or like the carpet of roses that Cleopatra spread for the officers of Mark Anthony.

Sooner or later God meets every trusting child who is following Him up the mountain and says, "Now prove that you believe this that you have told Me you believe, and that you have taught others to believe." Then is your opportunity.

God knows, and you know, that there was always a hope in your heart that a certain way would not be yours. "Anything but that, Lord," had been your earnest prayer. And then, perhaps quite suddenly, you found your feet set on that way, that and no other. Do you still hold fast to your faith that He makes your way perfect?

It does not look perfect. It looks like a road that has lost its sense of direction: a broken road, a wandering road, a strange mistake. And yet, either it is perfect, or all that you have believed crumbles like a rope of sand in your hands. There is no middle choice between faith and despair. ❀

Amy Carmichael (1867-1951) was a missionary who labored in India for 56 years. She founded the Dohnavur Fellowship, which eventually became a large compound that included a hospital and a house of prayer, to provide care for needy children.

FOR FURTHER STUDY ON THIS TOPIC:

A CHANCE TO DIE
BY ELISABETH ELLIOT (FLEMING H. REVELL)

TOWARD JERUSALEM
BY AMY CARMICHAEL (CHRISTIAN LITERATURE CRUSADE)

AMMA: THE LIFE AND WORDS OF AMY CARMICHAEL
BY ELIZABETH SKOGLUND AND RUTH BELL GRAHAM (BAKER)

SpiritLed Woman
30-Day Devotional
Prayer & Revival

Contents

Dedication

*This devotional is dedicated to those passionate, determined
women who have tasted the Lord's goodness and
are satisfied with nothing less.*

*You have walked with God on the mountaintops as well as in the
valleys of life, and you know that He can be trusted with
every challenge and in every season. He is ever faithful.*

*You've come to know the unmistakable sound of His voice.
Your heart leaps in obedient response to His words.
You are content either to be among the multitudes offering up
your praise or to be alone with Him in reverent solitude.*

*As you study these pages, I trust that God's peace will surround
you and His Spirit will compel you to pursue Him and all
that He wants to bestow. I pray too that His presence in
your life will be sweeter and more evident each day.*

*Brenda J. Davis
Editor, SpiritLed Woman*

*"I run in the path of Your commands, for You have set my heart free"
Psalm 119:32, NIV.*

DAY 1

&

THE SECRET OF REVIVAL

Read 2 Chronicles 7:12–18

66 "What is the secret of revival?" a great revivalist was asked. "There is no secret," he replied. "Revival always comes in answer to prayer."

Before America can have a sweeping, Holy Ghost revival, there must be a revival of prayer. And before this revival of prayer can come, there must be a conviction of sin and an open confession of the same among all followers of Christ. All movements of the Spirit in the past, without exception, have been started as the initial outpouring upon the hundred and twenty in the upper room — by the force of intense, believing prayer. Whenever the early church prayed as related in the book of Acts, we find the Spirit miraculously poured out.

The Wesleyan Revival, like Pentecost, came in answer to persistent, prevailing prayer. The practice of the primitive Methodists was to pray from four to five o'clock in the morning, religiously, and from five to six o'clock every evening. The leaders and founders of Methodism themselves spent hours and even all night in an agony of importunate prayer and started revival fires wherever they preached the Word.

Sarah Foulkes Moore
July 1941

Writer of many articles and tracts, Sarah Foulkes Moore also edited the *Herald of His Coming.*

"God's Plan for Setting the World Aflame," *The Pentecostal Evangel* (magazine published by the General Council of the Assemblies of God).

Day 2

Revival May Not Be What You Expect

Read Matthew 7:7–12

When revival comes, many supernatural things happen that are strange to the religious or skeptical mind. At times God waits until His people are desperately hungry so they won't dismiss the food He offers them.

A few years ago as we ministered in Michigan, the Holy Spirit began to move in a powerful way. Though it looked chaotic, God was in control. I noticed the pastor standing alone in a corner, so I asked him if he was all right. "I have lost control of this, and I don't know what to do," he replied. I asked, "Have you been praying for revival?" His answer was an emphatic yes.

Then the Holy Spirit told me what to say to him. "God is giving you a little taste of revival in order for you to realize what you have been praying for. Often in revival, God takes over, doing what He wants. We have to keep out of His way and follow the Holy Spirit, so don't be afraid."

He smiled and visibly relaxed. Although the New Testament says, "Let all things be done decently and in order" (1 Cor. 14:40, KJV), we must realize that God's idea of "decently and in order" may be vastly different from ours.

Kathie Walters

David and Kathie Walters, originally from England, focus their ministry on training children and teens to be strong in the Holy Spirit. They reside in Macon, Georgia, with their two daughters.

Living in the Supernatural (Macon, Ga.: Good News Fellowship Ministries, 1993), 62–63. Used by permission.

DAY 3

—————— ❧ ——————

UNITY IN PRAYER

Read Philippians 1

Unity in prayer has turned the tide in national crises. For example, England is acknowledged by historians to have been saved, through the ministry of John Wesley and his associates, from a similar bloody revolution as that which swept through France.

In 1738 Wesley went to a Moravian prayer meeting where he heard Peter Boler unfolding the book of Ephesians. Something happened. Later, Wesley wrote: "While Peter Boler taught, I felt my heart strangely warmed, and I could then and there for the first time say assuredly that my sins were forgiven through Jesus Christ my Lord."

That "little Moravian prayer meeting" lasted a hundred years. Bishop Hasse wrote that the great outpouring of the Spirit among the Moravians during the eighteenth century was the greatest since Pentecost. "Was there ever in the whole church history such an astonishing prayer meeting as that which, beginning at Herrnhut in 1727, went on one hundred years?"

Sarah Foulkes Moore
November 1936

Writer of many articles and tracts, Sarah Foulkes Moore also edited the *Herald of His Coming.*

The Pentecostal Evangel (magazine published by the General Council of the Assemblies of God).

3

DAY 4

❧

STEPS OF REVIVAL

Read Revelation 5:8, 8:3-4

After the revolution of 1775, America was in an unprecedented moral slum. Out of a population of five million, there were three hundred thousand confirmed drunkards. Shocking profanity was heard on the street, and bank robberies occurred daily.

By 1794 conditions reached their worst. A Baptist minister named Isaac Backus had an encounter with the Holy Spirit that convinced him of a national need for prayer. He sent a pamphlet to ministers of every denomination, pleading with them to open their churches for prayer all day on the first Monday of each month. The pastors and the people responded.

Revival began in 1798 in New England, where churches were unable to accommodate the large numbers of people inquiring about salvation. It finally exploded in the Great Revival of 1800 centered in Cane Ridge, Kentucky. Eleven thousand people flocked to this camp meeting (Kentucky's largest city, Lexington, had a population of only eighteen hundred!) The spiritual face of the nation was changed.

Let's retrace the steps of this revival: 1. A solitary individual had an encounter with the Holy Spirit. 2. A solitary individual initiated the effort. 3. A united prayer emphasis developed. 4. Revival came.

Burning, believing, prevailing, persuading, persevering, intimate prayer always precedes a move of God.

Alice Smith

Alice Smith is prayer coordinator for the U.S. Prayer Track of the A.D. 2000 & Beyond Movement.

Beyond the Veil (Ventura, Calif.: Regal, 1997), 24.

DAY 5

❧

REVIVAL IS COMING!

Read John 17

It was a time of spiritual death and unfavorable conditions when the great revival of 1857 broke out in New York City. People were so occupied with the affairs of this life that they were not interested in spiritual things.

Nevertheless, God had His praying man — someone who pressed into the Spirit because of the sins of the unrighteous. One single man — a layman, not a minister of the gospel — was so burdened for the people that he called a noonday prayer meeting, and when the time came he went to the appointed place and prayed. For half an hour he prayed alone until others dropped in. Six composed the first prayer meeting.

Interest grew from day to day until other places were opened for prayer throughout the city. As it gathered momentum, nearly every hamlet and community in the nation felt the quickening effect of the prayer meetings, and the influence extended even to other shores. Hundreds of thousands were brought to Christ in what was perhaps the most widespread visitation ever known on this continent.

Louise Nankivell
December 1944

Louise Nankivell was an evangelist with the Voice of Healing. She preached in sackcloth when conducting healing and evangelistic crusades, and many miracles took place in her meetings.

"Revival Is Coming," *The Pentecostal Evangel* (magazine published by the General Council of the Assemblies of God).

DAY 6

❧

REVIVAL FIRES SPREAD

Read James 5:13–18

In Calcutta, India, Dr. R. A. Torrey addressed a group of missionaries. Two of the ladies present were so impressed with the importance he placed upon intense, believing prayer that they returned to their mission station and prevailed upon their people to seek the Lord in prayer. Soon a great many in the district were on their knees crying out to God. Revival was inevitable, and within a short time eight thousand souls were saved.

Hearing of the marvelous story of India's revival, missionaries in Korea decided to pray every day until a similar revival was poured out on them. "After we had prayed for about a month," said one of the missionaries, "a brother proposed that we stop . . . The majority of us, however, decided that instead . . . we would give more time to prayer, not less. We changed the hour from noon to four o'clock in the morning. We kept at it until at last, after several months, the answer came." And what an answer! Over five hundred thousand Koreans were swept into the kingdom on the flood tide of this revival!

Sarah Foulkes Moore
July 1941

Writer of many articles and tracts, Sarah Foulkes Moore also edited the *Herald of His Coming.*

"God's Plan for Setting the World Aflame," *The Pentecostal Evangel* (magazine published by the General Council of the Assemblies of God).

DAY 7

❧

BROKEN CISTERNS

Read Mark 11:22–24; John 14:13–14; 1 John 5:14–15

God amazed me several years ago when He showed me that many people involved in the charismatic movement had turned to "broken cisterns" instead of to Him. Because of the abundant outpouring of good teaching, people were purchasing tapes and books and attending seminars to learn more about God's power, His ways, and what He was doing on earth at that time. Tapes and books and conferences are good! (In fact, you're reading a book right now that hopefully will encourage you as you seek to draw more closely to God.)

But the Lord showed me that His people were substituting other sources for spending time in prayer, waiting on Him. Sometimes it is so easy to hear from others about God and what He is doing that we don't bother to come to Him to find out what He wants to say to us. We don't bother to commune with Him and receive the life-giving Word for ourselves. Then we draw from broken cisterns. And the water from cisterns is never as fresh and pure as the water from God's moving, flowing, life-giving fountain.

Roxanne Brandt
1973

Roxanne Brandt was an international author and speaker in the charismatic movement. She conducted miracle services and crusades throughout the world.

Ministering to the Lord (Springdale, Pa.: Whitaker House, 1973). Used by permission.

7

DAY 8

❧

RECIPE FOR REVIVAL

Read 2 Chronicles 7:13–14; Joel 2–3

The prophet Joel called for the people to fast. This was not just a call to prayer, but to pray and fast, and for ministers to weep between the porch and the altar (see Joel 2:17). No church is going to see revival unless the ministers get down on their faces with the people and admit that they are bankrupt . . . until they admit that they are powerless and haven't got what they are professing to have. That is the recipe for revival.

God cannot help anyone until each person comes to the end of himself. He can't help until people come to the end of their sermon-making and to the end of playing church.

When we come to the end of ourselves, then God can move! If we do this, then God says He will leave us a blessing behind. As the prophet Joel wrote, God has promised that He will pour out His Spirit and that His sons and His daughters would prophesy. The latter-day rain! Revival!

Myrtle D. Beall
1950

Myrtle Beall was pastor and founder of Bethesda Missionary Temple in Detroit, Michigan, where the Latter Rain movement started in 1948.

"Recipe for Revival," from a wire recording of a radio program.

DAY 9

SIX ASPECTS OF PRAYER

(PART I)

Read verses listed below

Every form of prayer has its necessary function, thus we need to understand the Holy Spirit's desire for the six aspects of prayer.

1. *Petition* (Phil. 4:6; James 4:2–3; John 16:23–24). The Scriptures clearly teach that we must bring our requests for things we need to God, but we must be careful to watch our motivation for asking. We need to be in agreement with the Holy Spirit in what we are asking, and our requests need to promote the kingdom of God and His will and purpose for our lives or for the lives of those people for whom we are petitioning God.

2. *Thanksgiving* (Ps. 92:1; Ps. 100:4; 1 Thess. 5:18; 2 Tim. 3:1–2; Eph. 5:20). The psalmist taught us that thanksgiving is the proper way to enter the presence of God. Our thanksgiving is to be a genuine thankfulness to the Lord for what He has done for us; for His mercy, His grace, His longsuffering, and His goodness to us.

3. *Supplication* (Ps. 28:2; Acts 1:14; 4:31; 12; 1 Tim. 2:1–2). Supplication applies specifically to the humble and earnest cry that comes from the deep desire of the spirit and soul. The Holy Spirit gives us these deep cries and yearnings for the will of God to be fulfilled in our lives and in the lives of others.

(Continued on next day)

DAY 10

❧

SIX ASPECTS OF PRAYER

(PART II)

Read verses listed below

4. *Intercession* (Heb. 7:25; Rom. 8:26–27). This is the prayer of standing in the gap for someone else. Intercession is not a special ministry for only a few. Everyone who walks with the Holy Spirit knows intercession as He burdens their hearts for the needs of others. Many lives and churches have been snatched from the burning fire by the prayers of faithful intercessors.

5. *Praise* (Ps. 100:4). In praise we turn our eyes to God and away from ourselves. We praise him for who He is and for His mighty acts toward the sons of men.

6. *Worship* (Rev. 5:14; John 4:23). Worship occurs when our spirits have experienced a divine encounter with the living God. The Hebrew word for worship, *shachah*, can be translated as "bow down, crouch, do reverence, prostrate, and beseech humbly." The most used Greek word for worship in the New Testament is *proskuneo*, which means "to kiss toward." Worship is a heart's response to the manifest presence of God.

Fuchsia Pickett

Fuchsia Pickett has earned doctorates in both theology and divinity. After a miraculous healing from a genetic, life-threatening disease in 1959, she was baptized in the Holy Spirit and began to minister worldwide.

Presenting the Holy Spirit (Lake Mary, Fla.: Creation House, 1997), 162–167.

DAY 11

❧

FERVENT PRAYER

Read James 5:16

James says the "effectual fervent prayer of a righteous man availeth much." It is one thing to say a prayer, and quite another to pray a prayer — to prevail in prayer with God. Prevailing prayer leads us to a nearness with God. We get intimate and stand in holy awe before God.

Prevailing prayer conquered Esau and stopped the mouths of the lions when Daniel was in the lions' den. Elijah prevailed with God, and it rained not for three-and-a-half years. Again, he prayed, and there was great rain. Esther prayed the prayer of faith for her people, the Jews, and they were delivered from Haman.

The prayer of faith and fastings bring the power of God. Bloody Mary (Mary Queen of Scots) said, "I fear the prayers of John Knox more than all the armies of Europe." Her death warrant was signed in heaven as John Knox cried, "Give me Scotland or I die!" Martin Luther also prevailed with God when the emperor of Germany resolved to proclaim religious tolerance. Luther exclaimed, "Deliverance has come; deliverance has come." When the church of Christ as a body gets down to this kind of prayer, we will see the gifts brought back more fully and see the world brought to Christ.

Mrs. Ida McCoy
n.d.

Mrs. Ida McCoy was a minister closely associated with the Church of God Cleveland, Tennessee.

Neglected Themes and Helpful Hints (n.p., n.d.).

DAY 12

❧

PRAYER OF AGREEMENT

Read Matthew 18:19

"**A**gain I say to you that if two of you agree on earth concerning anything that they ask, it will be done for them by My Father in heaven" (Matt. 18:19, NKJV).

The prayer of agreement is one of the most powerful weapons that can be used in prayer. Agreement can be likened to filling a bottle with water. One person may pour in 20 percent, another 30 percent, still another 10 percent, and the last person 40 percent. When the bottle is filled or overflowing, then agreement is complete and the task is finished.

This is an important principle to know because some feel their prayers are so small they do not amount to very much. The truth is that those little prayers may make up the one percent that is lacking for the bottle to be full.

Some use the fact that many others are praying as an excuse not to be fervent in their prayers. Remember, in God's symphony each instrument is an integral part of the whole. If you don't pray when it's your time to intercede, God will move upon someone else to fill the gap, but it may delay His purposes and timing.

Cindy Jacobs

Cindy Jacobs is president of Generals of Intercession and advisor-at-large for Women's Aglow Fellowship. She and her family live in Colorado Springs.

Possessing the Gates of the Enemy (Grand Rapids, Mich.: Chosen Books, 1994), 93–94. Used by permission.

DAY 13

"THY WILL BE DONE..."

Read Matthew 6:6–15; 1 John 5:14–15

Have you been brought to a place of lowliness and submission, where "Thy will be done" seems the only desirable expression of prayer? Then press on in prayer to have God's will made clear, that you may know what Christ is longing for, and His own longing shall take possession of your own heart. Then there will be new meaning to the words, "What things soever ye desire, when ye pray, believe that ye receive them, and ye shall have them" (Mark 11:24, KJV).

Having no longer any doubt about the will of God in each matter of prayer, you will be able to press your claim boldly and to "believe that you take" (literal translation) "whatsoever ye desire." The same thoughts are brought out in 1 John 5:14–15: "If we ask anything according to his will, he heareth us: And if we know that he hear us, whatsoever we ask, we know that we have the petitions that we desired of him" (KJV).

Carrie Judd Montgomery
September 1943

Carrie Judd Montgomery was a writer, minister, missionary, and publisher. Beginning in 1881, she published a magazine for the next sixty-five years. She was active in many groups, including Christian Missionary Alliance, The Salvation Army, and the Assemblies of God.

"The Desires of Thine Heart," *The Pentecostal Evangel* (magazine published by the General Council of the Assemblies of God).

DAY 14

❦

PRAYING THROUGH

Read Genesis 28:10–16

If you need to pray through about something, stay in the presence of God, in prayer, until you get through to Him. God will reveal Himself. He will talk to you . . . but maybe not the first time; I should say not!

Just lately, I had to have a yes or no from God. I could have made my own plans and said, "This is what I want and this is what I'm going to do." But I can't operate like that; I want to hear God. I have to know that I am moving in the will of God, and when I know I'm in God's will He will give me His Word and anoint me by His Spirit. Then I can get somewhere with God.

Because I had to have a word from God (and the devil knew it), I said, "I don't care how long it takes! I'm going to stay here! I absolutely refuse to give an answer to this question until I hear from God!"

Hattie Hammond
n.d.

Called the "girl evangelist" because of the healings that took place in her meetings as a young woman, Hattie Hammond was considered one of the most intense speakers in the Pentecostal movement by the 1930s.

Audiocassette titled "How to Pray," from a chapel service at Christ for the Nations.

DAY 15

※

GUIDE TO PRAYING THROUGH

Read Colossians 4:2

Praying through is persistence in prayer until we have the assurance from God that His will has been accomplished in the earth realm.

One of the most often asked questions by those just beginning to pray through on the behalf of others is, "How do I know when I have prayed enough?" Here are several ways:

1. When the Holy Spirit no longer reminds us to pray. God will continue to prompt until His will is accomplished.

2. When we try to pray about a certain matter and there is absolutely no desire to pray. In other words, you have no unction from the Holy Spirit for more prayer. We may or may not see the answer in the natural at this point.

3. When God leads us to Scriptures that tell us victory is won.

4. When circumstances in the natural indicate the matter is taken care of, for example, the person is healed or restored.

Cindy Jacobs

Cindy Jacobs is president of Generals of Intercession and advisor-at-large for Women's Aglow Fellowship. She and her family live in Colorado Springs.

Possessing the Gates of the Enemy (Grand Rapids, Mich.: Chosen, 1994), 96–97. Used by permission.

DAY 16

❧

THE ANSWER IS ON THE WAY

Read Luke 22:39–46

One afternoon I felt a heavy burden to pray. I began to travail greatly in the Spirit, and it did not lift. The next week I stayed before the Lord and a great deal of the time prayed with such fervency that I knew I was touching God. Many times I would groan in the Spirit, and others would lay hands on me, but I had no relief. All I could do was pray.

It seemed the eyes of the Lord were looking right through me. I knew I must seek Him until I found relief. Then, after this had lasted for a week, I asked my husband to pray for me, and peace came into my spirit. Then in a vision I saw Jesus in the distance, kneeling. I could clearly see His soft brown hair as He knelt beside a rock — resembling a picture I had seen of Him kneeling in Gethsemane. I began to rejoice in the Spirit, as the Lord said to me, "All week you have been in Gethsemane." I knew then that the answer was on the way.

The following Sunday the power of God began to fall, souls were saved and filled, and bodies healed. It all began through intercessory prayer.

Carmen Thacker Goodwin
1992

Wife of Assemblies of God pastor J. R. Goodwin, Carmen was known for her unique teaching on the gifts of the Spirit.

Springtime and Harvest (Broken Arrow, Okla.: Self-published, 1992).

DAY 17

&

THE PRAISE ZONE

Read Psalm 86:12–17; Mark 11:24

If we ask God to give us a certain answer to prayer and proceed to believe we have it, it is only polite to begin to thank Him for it. In other words, shoot straight upward through the prayer zone into the praise zone, and thank God beforehand that according to His Word, it is done.

When contending with sickness, trouble, misunderstanding, discouragement, or depression, begin to see Jesus. Praise Him with all your heart, and the upward flight of His praises will lift you as with the wings of a great eagle above the woes of this earth.

Aimee Semple McPherson
1923

After being widowed in 1910 as a missionary in Hong Kong, Aimee Semple McPherson returned to ministry in the United States and eventually established the Foursquare denomination.

"Praising the Lord," *This Is That* (Self-published, 1923).

DAY 18

❧

WILL TO PRAY

Read Matthew 6:1–8

When you really "will to pray," find a closet and enter in — and pray. Don't just say prayers; pray! Your will enters into this thing. If you really will to pray and get through to God in prayer, the minute you say it, all hell comes up against you.

Before you can get on your knees, the telephone rings. Before you can begin, the devil attacks your mind with suggestions: "You ought to do this," or "You ought to do that!" "You'd better take care of this right now!" All that is pure devil!

There have been times when I have had to stomp my foot and say, "Devil, go to hell where you belong!" That's strong language, but you have to treat the devil like the devil — especially when your will is to pray!

Hattie Hammond
n.d.

Called the "girl evangelist" because of the healings that took place in her meetings as a young woman, Hattie Hammond was considered one of the most intense speakers in the Pentecostal movement by the 1930s.

Audiocassette titled "How to Pray," from a chapel service at Christ for the Nations.

DAY 19

❧

SATAN'S TERRITORY

Read Luke 10:19

As long as we are in Satan's territory — the world — he will try to attack us. For this reason, we should constantly ask God to cover us and surround us with the blood of Jesus. Then we must believe that Satan cannot harm us because of the blood. Jesus said, "I give unto you power . . . over all the power of the enemy" (Luke 10:19, KJV). This is the power of the blood of Jesus Christ, and by faith in His blood, to which we testify. The blood and the Word are all-powerful, but it takes true faith to set this never-failing power to work.

Use the blood and the Word against the enemy whenever he attacks you in spirit, soul, or body, and know that these take all power from the enemy. Also know that the enemy cannot put anything on you or keep anything from you, because God, who cannot lie, says the blood and the Word overcome Satan every time.

Mrs. C. Nuzum
1928

A missionary to Mexico, Mrs. C. Nuzum wrote a series of tracts later compiled as *The Life of Faith* that is still published by Gospel Publishing House.

The Life of Faith (Springfield, Mo.: Gospel Publishing House, 1928, 1996). Used by permission.

DAY 20

❧

REVELATION IN PRAYER

Read Psalm 1:1–2; 2 Timothy 3:16–17

Much of the time we spend in prayer with God each day should be devoted to quietly meditating on the Word and allowing the Holy Spirit to speak to our hearts. Revelation comes from the Holy Spirit, who dwells within us.

Each time God gives us fresh insight into the Word, He makes the *logos* (the written Word) become *rhema* (a living word) to our spirits. Just as the Holy Spirit caused Mary to conceive in her physical body, so the Holy Spirit can impregnate our spirits with the living Word. Reading the Scriptures in communion with the Holy Spirit, who is the Author, causes them to live in our spirits.

Spiritual, mental, and physical renewal come to us because we wait in prayer on the Holy Spirit. The Holy Spirit transforms our minds to think God's thoughts, and we come into harmony with the will of God. It is the Holy Spirit who then anoints us to minister with power and authority that revealed Word of God to others.

Fuchsia Pickett

Fuchsia Pickett has earned doctorates in both theology and divinity. After a miraculous healing from a genetic, life-threatening disease in 1959, she was baptized in the Holy Spirit and began to minister worldwide.

Presenting the Holy Spirit (Lake Mary, Fla.: Creation House, 1997), 13–14.

Day 21

Faith Comes With Hope

Read Proverbs 13:12; 1 Corinthians 13:13

Proverbs 13:12 says, "Hope deferred makes the heart sick, but a desire fulfilled is a tree of life" (RSV). Is your hope put off right now? Is your heart sick from waiting?

The will of God is not based on your situation. Be aggressive in your faith to believe God because if He told you He will do something, you can be sure He will do it. Don't start looking for your own solution to your problems.

You worry for fear you may do the wrong thing. You wonder, *Should I confess it, lay it down, speak it or crucify it?* The answer is to do all these things and then stand on His word. Confess your promise and take authority over the doubt and unbelief from the enemy. Get into the presence of the Father, and tell Him He is more important than the promise.

The Bible says, "Now abide faith, hope and love" (1 Cor. 13:13, NKJV). You have already heard faith and love preached over and over again. Let me remind you to hold on to your hope. Faith only comes with hope.

Cathy Lechner

Cathy Lechner is known for her powerful prophetic ministry as well as her teaching. She, her husband, and a house full of children (many adopted) live in Jacksonville, Florida.

I'm Trying to Sit at His Feet, but Who's Going to Cook Dinner? (Lake Mary, Fla.: Creation House, 1995), 24–25.

DAY 22

❧

ASKING FOR DIRECTION

Read 1 Samuel 14:18–23, 14:36–15:29; Psalm 16:11

Before Saul entered into the first war with the Philistines, he went to the priest and asked him to get the ark of God. Before Saul had finished talking to the priest, God had moved on Saul's behalf and confused the Philistines so that they were striking each other with swords. Saul and his army went out to battle and obtained the victory (see 1 Sam. 14:18–23).

But that was the last time Saul conferred with a godly spiritual authority before making a decision. Nevertheless, God gave Saul many other victories in battles, even though Saul battled on his own terms. Saul's self-reliance and arrogance finally led him to disobedience and rebellion against God, and God later rejected him (see 1 Sam. 14:36–15:29). Like so many of us who experience success at something and then decide we know how to do it from that point on, Saul stopped asking for God's guidance after his first victory.

There are many churches and ministries today that have risen with step-by-step directions from the Lord until they reached a place of success. Then their leaders stopped inquiring of the Lord. Surprisingly, when such churches begin to stagnate or go downhill, the leaders seem genuinely baffled. They don't understand that in ministry, as well as in marriages and individual lives, one thing is true: If you stop asking for God's guidance, you stop receiving it.

Iverna Tompkins

With a special emphasis on training leaders, Iverna Tompkins has ministered as a speaker and writer for many years. She is the sister of popular author Judson Cornwall.

All in God's Time (Lake Mary, Fla.: Creation House, 1996), 99–100.

Day 23

❧

Personal Prayer Partners

Read Ephesians 6:19–22

Today it seems ministers are experiencing serious attack and going through much turmoil. Many who have been respected as mentors are having serious problems. Those who are still surviving the attack cry out, "How can I keep these things from happening to me?"

Whenever those in ministry call me with a burden, I ask, "Do you have personal prayer partners?" They invariably reply, "I have people who pray for me on a regular basis." And I say, "But do they know your needs on an intimate level?" Only a handful of leaders can say yes to that question.

Is it biblical to have personal intercessors? Yes. Over and over at the close of his letters Paul asked churches to pray for him and told them his needs. He also sent Tychicus to the church of Ephesus specifically that they might know of Paul's affairs and pray for him (Eph. 6:19–22).

You don't have to be in a public ministry to need prayer! Every intercessor needs the support of a prayer partner.

Cindy Jacobs

Cindy Jacobs is president of Generals of Intercession and advisor-at-large for Women's Aglow Fellowship. She and her family live in Colorado Springs.

Possessing the Gates of the Enemy (Grand Rapids, Mich.: Chosen Books, 1991), 157.

DAY 24

MOBILIZING CHILDREN FOR PRAYER

Read Mark 10:13–16

Children and teenagers often limit their prayer experience to a few short minutes of praying over meals or special prayer requests while planning some fun endeavor. Their prayers often go like this: "Lord, please give us a good sunny day when we go to the beach tomorrow, and make Becky's mother let her come. And may we have a real fun time."

Although these prayers are legitimate, they tend to be what we would call the selfish prayer. We need to encourage our youngsters to know what it means to really travail in prayer for the lost and to pray in the Holy Spirit (Jude 20). They must learn how to intercede for others (Eph. 6:18).

Most youngsters have many friends and acquaintances who are either non-Christians or are not walking with the Lord. We suggest that you organize your youngsters into "witnessing teams." With the team concept, when the children are at school or in the neighborhood, they will realize they are not alone but are part of an army of young prayer warriors who are agreeing with them for their friends to be saved. As they work together and support each other in prayer, they will see results they never dreamed possible (James 5:16–18; Mark 11:24).

Kathie Walters

David and Kathie Walters, originally from England, focus their ministry on training children and teens to be strong in the Holy Spirit. They reside in Macon, Georgia, with their two daughters.

David and Kathie Walters, *Kids in Combat* (Macon, Ga.: Good News Fellowship Ministries, 1989), 78–79.

DAY 25

A SECRET SOURCE OF STRENGTH

Read Psalm 81

There is a secret source of strength for this battle we are engaged in, which we will be wise to avail ourselves of constantly. It is in communing with Jesus.

Holding a feast with Him in our hearts, worshiping Him, loving Him, adoring Him, conscious of His presence continually — here is the instrument perfectly adjusted to the Master's touch. The emptied vessel is filled with the constantly inflowing and outflowing water of life. His breath is our breath. The life that flows in the Head of the body is the life that flows in the veins of the body, and this walk of communion is a conscious reality to us. Our eyes are not on the waves at our feet, but they rest on the face of Jesus.

Distractions and distresses come in only when our gaze falls. When we look down at the sea of life over which we are walking — restless, unstable, changing — that restlessness seizes us. We are perplexed and beaten about by waves. We are sinking out of our element. We do not belong in that sea. Those waves should concern us little. Our walk is above them.

Zelma E. Argue
October 1921

Zelma Argue was a Canadian born evangelist and teacher in the Pentecostal movement and the daughter of A. H. Argue.

"Communion With Jesus," *The Pentecostal Evangel* (magazine published by the General Council of the Assemblies of God).

Day 26

❧

Fellowship With the Holy Spirit

Read John 16:12–13

Once we have accepted the Holy Spirit as a divine Person, we can learn to enjoy intimate communion with Him as we give ourselves to prayer and fellowship with Him. There is a difference between having fellowship with the Spirit and merely interacting with Him to perform a specific task. For example, we may sense an anointing to preach the Word or receive discernment of spiritual things even though we are not walking in fellowship with Him as He intended.

Many of us still think of the Holy Spirit coming into our lives as merely an experience of power that brought spiritual gifts. In reality, the Holy Spirit comes into our lives as a person, not as an experience. Walking in fellowship with the Holy Spirit requires spending time with Him, allowing Him to talk to us. As we do, we learn to become sensitive to His moods, which reveal His desires in a particular situation or for a person. And we will learn what pleases Him in even the small issues of our everyday life.

Fuchsia Pickett

Fuchsia Pickett has earned doctorates in both theology and divinity. After a miraculous healing from a genetic, life-threatening disease in 1959, she was baptized in the Holy Spirit and began to minister worldwide.

Presenting the Holy Spirit (Lake Mary, Fla.: Creation House, 1997), 12–13.

DAY 27

❧

THIS IS FOR YOU

Read Luke 10:38–42

I was a "Martha mom." I neglected myself spiritually, always giving out and never taking in. This neglect was not for spiritual gain, but for mommy busyness. I'd get down on the floor to pray and notice a Lego under the sofa. Soon I was cleaning the entire upstairs, totally forgetting I had kneeled down to pray.

Sometimes we just have to let the Legos lie, close our eyes, and press in to God. At first this may seem more difficult than cleaning. Women are used to activity. That's how we feel needed. Martha wanted Mary in the kitchen laboring over the food preparation. Mary had the attitude, "I can eat later; right now Jesus is talking, and I want to hear Him."

I used to view prayer as just one more thing I had not accomplished by the end of my day. I did pray every day, but I wanted to have two full hours in the closet (which I'm sure I would have begun to straighten). At the end of the day when I was finally able to squeeze in a few minutes with God, I thought He was upset because I hadn't given Him two hours earlier in the day, so I would spend my prayer time apologizing. One day He interrupted my condemnation report. "This is for you!" He said. "Stop seeing Me as angry at you for not coming earlier. I am glad we are together now. Let Me refresh you so you will look forward to these times together." This revolutionized my outlook on prayer.

Lisa Bevere

Lisa Bevere is an author and minister who lives in Orlando, Florida, with her husband and four sons.

Out of Control and Loving It! (Lake Mary, Fla.: Creation House, 1996), 154–155.

DAY 28

WHAT THE DEVIL FEARS

Read Acts 26:16–18

The devil fears nothing like prayer. He knows that if he can break our communication with God, he has cut us off from all power. Hence, he sentinels the gateway of prayer with his seducing agents. He deadens the spiritual sensibilities, hatches excuses, makes evasions in the mind, causes us to suddenly grow dull and drowsy and indolent, and in a thousand other ways he works untiringly to keep us from getting hold of God in earnest prayer.

He engineers strange circumstances to keep us from our knees. He incites a false zeal and, in a multitude of church activities, crowds out prayer. To the degree that he succeeds in causing us to neglect prayer, he has won the day. Our victory comes in arousing and stirring up all the faculties of taking hold of God in the combats of prayer.

Sarah Foulkes Moore
October 1936

Writer of many articles and tracts, Sarah Foulkes Moore also edited the *Herald of His Coming*.

"Revival Follows Prayer," *The Pentecostal Evangel* (magazine published by the General Council of the Assemblies of God).

DAY 29

❧

THE SECRET PLACE

Read Psalm 91

There is a secret place within the holy of holies under the very cover of Christ's wing — a place where we always have access to the mercy seat. It's a place of unbroken communion; a place where our spirits are made so spotless by the blood of Jesus that He can always smile upon us. This is the "secret place of the Most High." This is the life hid with Christ in God.

Some of you have at last come to a difficulty that you felt even God could not meet, and in your unbelief you did not know Him as the One who had all might. That was because you were not abiding in the secret place of the Most High.

Oh, Beloved! Let us not be satisfied with anything short of this: There is a holy place, but there is also a holy of holies. If you are not satisfied with anything less, God will give you His uttermost salvation.

Carrie Judd Montgomery
October 1940

Carrie Judd Montgomery was a writer, minister, missionary, and publisher. Beginning in 1881, she published a magazine for the next sixty-five years. She was active in many groups, including Christian Missionary Alliance, The Salvation Army, and the Assemblies of God.

Triumphs of Faith (published by Carrie Judd Montgomery).

DAY 30

❧

THE GREATEST BATTLE

Read Romans 7:23–25, 8

Sometimes you have the greatest battle with the enemy when you get on your knees and mean real business with God. Some mornings I have gone into my room and waited, and as I have tried to get my mind on God, it seemed as though it went around like a phonograph record. I thought of everything and everybody in the world.

That's all right; God is dealing with you, trying to draw you to Himself. The old flesh is kicking and pulling and drawing from the other side. But God is pulling too, so wait. Just be quiet. He is there; He is waiting. He sees you on your knees, but He wants to know whether you mean business. And when you prove you mean business, and stay there, lay hold of God. You are sure to get something from Him. The world is looking for reality. The world wants to see reality in the lives of professing men and women. They are standing at our church doors and crying through our windows. Shall we not be still before God until our souls are filled and flooded and saturated again with God? Then we shall see revival.

Hattie Hammond
August 1928

Called the "girl evangelist" because of the healings that took place in her meetings as a young woman, Hattie Hammond was considered one of the most intense speakers in the Pentecostal movement by the 1930s.

"Drawing Nigh to God," *The Pentecostal Evangel* (magazine published by the General Council of the Assemblies of God).